Samuel Keene, one of the first members of the LCTA

FOOD FOR MAN AND BEAST

Other books by Hugh Barty-King

SUSSEX IN 1839

SCRATCH A SURVEYOR

ROUND TABLE, THE SEARCH FOR FELLOWSHIP

THE BALTIC EXCHANGE

A TRADITION OF ENGLISH WINE

HUGH BARTY-KING

Food for Man and Beast

The story of the London Corn Trade Association,
the London Cattle Food Trade Association and
the Grain and Feed Trade Association

1878–1978

HUTCHINSON BENHAM
LONDON

Hutchinson Benham Limited
3 Fitzroy Square, London W1P 6JD

An imprint of the Hutchinson Group

London Melbourne Sydney Auckland
Wellington Johannesburg and agencies
throughout the world

First published 1978

© Text and illustrations The Grain and Feed Trade Association 1978

Set in Monotype Bembo

Printed in Great Britain by The Anchor Press Ltd
and bound by Wm Brendon & Son Ltd
both of Tiptree, Essex

ISBN 0 09 133480 2

Contents

Illustrations

The President of the Grain and Feed Trade Association,
Mr Donald McLachlan Clark

Foreword

Donald M. McLachlan Clark
President of GAFTA

It is a great honour to be President of GAFTA in this the cen-
tenary year of the London Corn Trade Association and to present
this short history of our Association and, more particularly, of our
predecessors. It is a still continuing story of service to the trade
after many vicissitudes, in particular two World Wars, and
through many changes in commercial traditions and techniques.
In 1971, the services and traditions of the LCTA and the Cattle
Food Trade Association were harmoniously joined together to
form GAFTA.

The Association depends on its members and I must pay tribute
to the long line of my predecessors who have given so much of
their time and energy over the years to serve the membership and
the trade, and to build up our predecessor associations and GAFTA
to what it is today

In this brief story reference is made to many aspects of our
work, for example, in time of war, our services to the government and at all times our efforts to make sure that proper regard
was given to the interests of the trade and proper consideration
given to our views, particularly on commercial matters. But if
there is one single common thread it is the concern to provide for
a trade, which by its nature is an international one, a common
framework for the conduct of that trade. Our predecessors first
came together to encourage uniformity in the commercial use of
forms of contract, to publish 'agreed forms of contract etc, and
urge their use throughout the trade'. That task remains as import-

ant as ever it was. Already, an increasingly large proportion of the world's trade in grain and feeding stuffs is transacted on GAFTA terms. The reason for this can be only that traders, actively engaged in the calculated risks of their professions, have recognized the importance of uniformity in limiting those risks. I would hope, therefore, that those who, understandably, may wish to establish their own national or local terms, would be guided by our experience and our history in establishing terms and conditions mutually satisfactory to all parties to a commercial transaction.

Ours is a trade that transcends frontiers both geographically and politically. It is in all our interests, as members of the international community, to ensure that it flows as smoothly as possible, and one way to achieve this is to use contract forms that are universally trusted, accepted and understood.

Acknowledgements

The author wishes to thank Mr James Mackie, Mr Michael Johnson and Mr George Saville for the help and advice given during the writing of this history, and to acknowledge the information derived from documents in the archives of the Baltic Exchange.

Whoever examines with attention the history of
the dearths and famines which have afflicted any
part of Europe, during either the course of the
present or that of the two preceding centuries, of
several of which we have pretty exact accounts, will
find, I believe, that a dearth has never arisen from
any combination among the inland dealers in corn,
nor from any other cause but a real scarcity,
occasioned sometimes perhaps, and in some particular
places, by the waste of war, but in by far the greatest
number of cases by the fault of the seasons: and that
a famine has never arisen from any other cause but the
violence of government attempting, by improper means,
to remedy the inconveniences of a dearth.

When the government, in order to remedy the
inconveniences of a dearth, orders all the dealers
to sell their corn at what it supposes a reasonable
price, it either hinders them from bringing it to
market, which may sometimes produce a famine even in
the beginning of the season: or if they bring it thither
it enables the people, and thereby encourages them, to
consume it so fast as must necessarily produce a famine
before the end of the season. The unlimited, unrestrained
freedom of the corn trade, as it is the only effectual
preventative of the miseries of a famine, so it is the
best palliative of the inconveniences of a dearth:
for the inconveniences of a real scarcity cannot be
remedied, they can only be palliated. No trade deserves
more the full protection of the law, and no trade requires
it so much, because no trade is so much exposed to popular
odium.

ADAM SMITH, Inquiry into the Nature and Causes
of the Wealth of Nations, 1776

CORN.

1.

THAT it is expedient that an Act, made in the 44th year of the Reign of His present Majesty, intituled, " An Act to regulate the Importation and " Exportation of Corn, and the Bounties and Duties payable thereon ;" and also an Act, made in the 45th year of the Reign of His present Majesty, for explaining and amending the said Act of the 44th year, be Repealed ; Except only so far as the said Act of the 44th year repeals any part of an Act, made in the 31st year of the Reign of His present Majesty, intituled, " An Act for the " regulating of the Importation and Exportation of Corn, and the payment of " the Duty on Foreign Corn imported, and of the Bounty on British Corn " exported."

2.—THAT it is expedient, that so much of the said Act of the 31st year of His present Majesty's reign, as regulates the Exportation of Corn from *Great Britain*, for victualling or providing any of His Majesty's Forces, Forts or Garrisons, or the Exportation of Corn to certain places from certain Ports in *Great Britain*, as described in the Table marked (C.) in the said Act ; and also so much of the said recited Act as prohibits the Exportation of Corn from *Great Britain*, be Repealed.

3.—THAT it is expedient, that so much and such parts of any Act or Acts, passed by the Parliament of *Ireland*, as regulate the Exportation or Importation of Corn, or as grant or allow any Duties or Bounties thereon, be Repealed.

4.—THAT it is expedient, that the Exportation of Corn and Grain, from any part of the United Kingdom, should be permitted, at all times, without the payment of any Duty, and without receiving any Bounty whatever.

5.—THAT it is expedient, that *Ireland* should be divided into Four maritime Districts, and Four inland Districts ; and that the prices of Corn and Grain, within them, should be taken and returned to the Receiver of Corn Returns, in like manner as in *England*.

6.—THAT it is expedient, that the Duty on the Importation of Corn, Grain and Flour, into any part of the United Kingdom, should be regulated by the aggregate average Price of Corn and Grain, in the whole of the Twelve maritime Districts of *England* and *Wales* ; the Four maritime Districts of *Scotland*; and the Four maritime Districts of *Ireland*.

7.—THAT it is expedient, that the Importation of Corn and Grain, into the United Kingdom, should be permitted, whatever the Price thereof may be in any part of the said United Kingdom ; subject only to the following Duty (that is to say) Whenever the average price of Wheat, Rye, Barley, Bere or Bigg, Oats, Pease or Beans, throughout the whole of the United Kingdom, shall exceed the total amount of the average price of each such Corn or Grain respectively, within *Great Britain*, for the 20 years ending on the 15th day of November then next preceding, together with a sum equal to One-fifth part of such average price added thereto, then and in such case a Duty shall be paid on the Importation of each such Corn or Grain respectively into any part of the United Kingdom, at and after the Rate of 1*s* for every Quarter of such Corn or

274.   Grain

The Corn Laws, June 1813

I

In nineteenth-century London, centre of the world grain trade, the LCTA fills a long-felt want
1898–1900

The haughty possess the land,
    And wield oppression's rod,
In spite of that divine command,
    Found in the word of God;
The Corn Laws petrify their hearts,
    And make the nation groan,
For when the people cry for bread,
    They only get a stone.

Then open every British port,
    And let the poor be fed,
No longer see your children starve,
    And die through want of bread.

The formal speeches of the haughty Duke of Richmond, The Farmers' Friend and President of the Society for the Protection of Agriculture, were no match for the popular songs of the Anti-Corn Law League. There was no need to take sides so long as British farmers grew enough corn to feed the whole of Britain's population, for then Charles II's Corn Laws, imposing levies on imported grain, had little effect. But, by the end of the Napoleonic Wars, it was clear that Great Britain was no longer capable of feeding a rapidly growing population from her own resources. Nonetheless, a parliament dominated by landlords was still able to maintain the price of domestic grain through the Corn Laws, until the opposition of the informed middle classes concerned at the growing misery of the poor, competition from foreign factories, and the total failure to prevent the disastrous Irish Famine of 1845, combined to secure their repeal.

Foremost in the agitation against the Corn Laws were the middle-class corn merchants whose activities began to be conducted on a scale worthy of being called a trade from the time import duties were lifted on foreign corn. 'Is this the country which can only flourish in the sickly artificial atmosphere of prohibition? Is this the country to stand shivering on the brink of exposure to the healthful breezes of competition?' asked Sir Robert Peel in the speech he made in the House of Commons on 16 February 1846 inviting members to repeal the outmoded legislation. Where there was no competition, there was no merchant.

Central and local government in Britain had for long regarded the provision of sufficient corn for breadmaking as a sacred trust, and in London the City Corporation and the livery companies saw fit to keep a store of grain in public granaries against the day when circumstances beyond their control produced a scarcity. But when the Great Fire of London destroyed the granaries in 1666, private trading took over and corn merchants appeared in Cheapside and Cornhill. At the beginning of the eighteenth century the Corn Market was in Bear Quay in Thames Street. In towns all over Britain a farmer who had grain to sell loaded it on to a waggon and sent it to market. One sack was thrown off the cart into the market place for millers to examine. The one who liked it placed an order, or if he was not satisfied with the 'sample', he walked along the line of waggons until he came to the one with the grain he had sampled and saw it in bulk.

As the scale of the buying and selling operation got too big for simple producer-to-consumer transactions of this kind, both parties were glad to entrust the commercial aspect of wheat growing or flour milling to a third party. The landlord of an inn in Whitechapel to whom Essex farmers gave samples of their corn to show to millers was probably the prototype corn merchant. Life had become less leisurely and farmers could not afford to wait until their prospective customers showed up. It paid them to

1. Perspective View of the CORN FACTORS EXCHANGE, erected in Mark Lane 1751.

The Corn Exchange, Mark Lane, 1751

give the innkeeper a commission on the orders he took. Soon men were ready to do this for a group of farmers full time, and the proliferation of such agents or factors necessitated a meeting place where they could exchange samples and information – the first corn exchange.

London merchants opened one in Mark Lane in 1749 beside the Old Ship Inn. It was rebuilt in 1827 and became the 'new corn exchange'. Another building put up a few years later remained unaltered and for that reason was known as the 'old corn exchange', though in fact it was the younger of the two.

A corn exchange was merely a domestic market, but the corn merchants of Liverpool who had built themselves a corn exchange in 1808 went one step further and formed themselves seven years after the repeal of the Corn Laws in 1846 into an association. Two years later Glasgow corn merchants, who had built a corn exchange in 1841, followed suit. The Liverpool Grain Trade Association of 1853 and the Glasgow Corn Trade Association of 1855 were the first in the field. They differed from the *club* which everyone called The Baltic which had started as a coffee house Subscription Room and had moved to new premises in South Sea House, Threadneedle Street, London, in 1857. The Baltic for long (since 1823) had been an association of grain dealers, and the floor of The Baltic a meeting place where brokers, buyers, sellers and shippers of grain could meet and strike bargains (though no samples were allowed).

For a corn merchant distribution of home-grown grain was a comparatively simple matter – collecting it from the farmer's gate and delivering it to the miller by horse and cart, doing a leisurely fifteen miles a day, or sending it down the coast by ship to London and thence by river and canal to the Midlands. But the merchant-ing function became more complicated once imported foreign grain, given a boost by the repeal of the Corn Laws, became the greater proportion of Britain's total consumption. Compared with a cart load, the quantity of grain carried in a ship's hold was enormous; instead of tens of tons, hundreds and then thousands. As economic forces created a demand for grain on a scale unheard of before, both for man and beast, and sources of supply kept changing, the constant factor was Britain's role as the corn market of the world, with London, its capital, at the centre of it all.

A big scale operation beyond their immediate financial resources forced those who became involved in the post-1846 corn trade to lean on London merchant bankers to finance bulk purchases of foreign wheat, persuading them, as best they knew how, to advance them funds against shipping documents. Bankers who found themselves dealing with a multiplicity of merchants, each of whom had his own form of contract and business usages, soon saw the need for standard practices throughout a trade which embraced not only Britain but countries far beyond. They demanded the inclusion of uniform clauses which would cover them in the event of the transaction going wrong. Foreign grain was shipped before it was sold. As soon as the ship put into Falmouth, corn factors swarmed on board to obtain samples of the cargo, take them to London and find a buyer. Instructions then went back to the ship regarding its final port of call which might be Amsterdam, Genoa or London. There were considerable risks involved, and to reduce them the merchant bankers who made the loans insisted that the phrasing of contracts was as watertight as the ships to which they entrusted their investment. For a long time sea navigation had been unduly hazardous, but it was becoming less so. The perfecting of steam propulsion and the invention of the electric telegraph helped to give the corn trade more precision and reliability than hitherto, and the City of London became more generous in their interest and insurance rates. Little could be done to protect the farmer from the effects of drought or flood, but science was fast coming to the aid of the ship's master and his owner in reducing journey time and the

The Corn Exchange, 1842

uncertainties of traversing the oceans. As the world's corn producers learnt to deposit more and more of their surplus wheat and barley on a Britain which they knew to be managing its own corn trade so successfully, commercial risks had to be carefully weighed – buy cheaply from the South American in need of cash and maybe have to store it at a high cost for many months if no immediate buyer could be found? Or lose an opportunity of making a quick sale at a higher price and an easy profit? Those who had to use their judgement as individual traders time after time, each so to speak out on a limb, felt increasingly vulnerable. By the 1870s they felt the need for a framework to contain the multiplicity of daily transactions and to give them form and pattern, which gave individual buyers and sellers a sense of belonging to a general activity in which they were all sharing. Important to the activity was the way foreign grain was handled at the point of entry, and it was essential that port practices should also be standardized, and in a way that took cognizance of technological changes in transport and communication.

Moreover, once Britain had become an international centre, and grain came in from an ever widening variety of sources, a merchant wanted to free himself from being committed to a single source with a limited margin and be able to have an option contract providing for an alternative source and trim the price. Above all everyone had to agree on the nomenclature, and to base their business on commonly accepted definitions of terms like Fair Average Quality (FAQ), and this meant uniform contracts.

All this pre-supposed a central, sophisticated organization, and it was to provide this that four leading corn merchants called a meeting at the Baltic Sale Room in the City of London on 15 May 1878 to discuss the formation of a 'London Corn Trade Association'. John Ross took the chair and John Kressman acted as honorary secretary. The two other prime movers were Richard Duck who agreed to become treasurer and William J. Harris.

The circular sent to corn merchants likely to be interested stated that the formation of such an association was a long-felt want. Its objects were to initiate any new form of contract which might appear necessary; to protect the interests of the corn trade generally; and to select from its members 'a limited number of gentlemen of matured judgement and honourable character with practical knowledge of the corn trade to act as a final Court of Appeal in Arbitrations'.

In reporting the meeting, *The Times* stated there was a crowded attendance. The proposed annual subscription was one guinea. Such an association, said John Ross, would be of national interest, not only to the corn trade of Great Britain but also to shipowners, insurance companies and Lloyds. The idea was supported by 'the most eminent firms in London', he said, but in fact there were quite a number who were opposed to it.

The main business of the meeting was formally to nominate fifty of their number to a General Committee. Their names had already been selected, and on a motion of John Kressman, seconded by Stephen Ralli, they were duly appointed. Of these seventeen were nominated as the Executive Committee who became the association's governing body. At the inauguration of the London Corn Trade Association on 31 May 1878 John Ross was elected Founder President and Marmaduke J. Cradock became the first Secretary. It had no headquarters and committee meetings were held in members' offices in turn. Founder firms included William Adams & Co, S. W. Keene & Co (still in business under this name), Ralli Brothers (still functioning as Ralli Maclaine Limited), Raymond & Reid, Usborne & Son (also still operating in 1978). The association's funds were not very large in those early days, and the legend grew up that Richard Duck carried them around with him in his pocket inside a paper bag.

The association's first contract form was for East Indian wheat. This was followed by a Black Sea and an American form.

The American Grain Contract began:

A Cargo of . . . fair average quality of the season's shipment at time and place of shipment. Shipment in good condition per . . . a first-class vessel (Turks excepted) classed not lower than A 1 in red English, 5/6 1 1 French Veritas, or equal classification in Austrian, Norwegian or Italian, or other equal register from . . . 10 per cent, more or less as per Bill or Bills of Lading dated . . . at the price of . . . say . . . per 480lbs shipped including Freight and Insurance to any safe port in the United Kingdom of Great Britain and Ireland, calling at Queenstown, Falmouth, or Plymouth for Orders, as per Charter Party; vessel to discharge afloat, no charge for Dunnage.

On the back were ten rules. Sufficient days were given for sailing vessels and steamers. Rule ten was the arbitration clause which said all disputes arising out of the contract should be referred to two arbitrators, one chosen by each party, and they had to be principals engaged in the corn trade as merchants, factors, or brokers and members of the London Corn Exchange or The Baltic.

When fifty members met for the first annual meeting on 13 May 1879 they were told of this and the two other contracts which the Committee had passed, East Indian Wheat and Black Sea ('Tale Quale' and 'Sea Damage'). Some of those who till now had drawn up their own contracts whose detail they considered superior to their rivals', were not easily won over to the drafting of a document which was meant to suit everyone. A Mr Valieri who was the spokesman of the Black Sea merchants objected to the phrase 'shipment in good order and condition' in the 'Sea Damage' clauses of the Black Sea Contract. He wanted a proviso added 'due allowance being made for season's crop and time of shipment'. He contended that a cargo arriving out of condition was no proof of it being shipped in bad condition. Stephen Ralli agreed that the buyer should have to bear the loss if the shipper, having done his duty in shipping good wheat, the cargo arrived out of condition. Edward Majolier said some sellers thought they had done their duty so long as they got the captain to sign for the cargo as in good condition. Seth Taylor of Waterloo Flour Mills insisted that the *bona fide* of the seller was the essence of the business; buyers were entirely in the hands of sellers. Mr Valieri, said William Harris, wanted to put in something which would enable bad shippers to father bad cargoes on the buyers in London. The seller must take back sea-damaged grain and claim from under-

London Corn Trade Association contract for American Grain Parcels, 1888

LONDON CORN TRADE ASSOCIATION.

AMERICAN GRAIN CONTRACT.
PARCELS.

No. 2. **1888.**

Per steamer or sailing vessel.

Entered at Stationers' Hall.

LONDON,..18...........

....

on the printed conditions and rules endorsed on this contract.

✠ of fair average quality of the season's shipments, at time and place of shipment.

✠ About as per sample marked.................................due allowance being made for handling and smallness of same.

Shipment, in good condition...

✠ per...classed not lower than A 1 in red English,
5/6 1 1 French Veritas, or equal classification in Austrian, Norwegian, Italian, or other equal register
(Greek and Turkish sailing vessels excepted).

✠ Per good grain carrying steamer...

from ....

As per Bill or Bills of Lading dated or to be dated..

....say..

....Units, 5 per cent. more or less,

at the price of..say...

per............lbs. shipped, including Freight and Insurance to...

The unit of quantity under this contract shall be..............lbs. English.

Should the above form part of a larger quantity loose collected damaged and sweepings to be shared *pro-rata.*
Vessel to discharge afloat and according to the custom of the Port.

If vessel be discharged on the Continent the out-turn to be computed at $50\frac{3}{4}$ kilos., equal to 112 lbs. English,
in French, Belgian, and Dutch Ports ; 1,016 kilos. equal to 2,240 lbs. English in German Ports.

Any deficiency on Bill of Lading weight to be paid for by Seller, and any excess over Bill of Lading weight
to be paid for by Buyer at contract price.

No payment shall be made for increase in weight occasioned by water during the voyage. In case of Sea
Accident causing a deficiency, Provisional Invoice to be final. Pumping up grain not to be considered a
Sea Accident.

Payment by cash in London in exchange for Shipping documents on or before arrival of Vessel at destination,
but in no case later than the prompt, less discount for the unexpired time of seventy-two days from date of
Bill or Bills of Lading, at the rate of one-half of one per cent. per annum above the advertised rate of interest
for short deposits allowed by the leading Joint Stock Banks in London, or (at Seller's option) by Buyer's
acceptances at equal thereto, with Shipping documents attached as usual.

Seller to give Policies $\frac{and}{or}$ Certificates of Insurance for two per cent. over the Invoice amount ; any amount
over this to be for Seller's account in case of total loss only. Insurance (free of war risk), to be effected (at
Seller's option) with approved American Underwriters or Companies paying losses, if any, on gold basis in
England, and on Lloyd's conditions, $\frac{and}{or}$ approved English Underwriters or Companies ; but for whose
solvency Seller is not to be responsible.

In case of prohibition of export, blockade, or hostilities preventing shipment, this Contract, or any unfulfilled
part thereof, shall be at an end.

Seller to pay.................Brokerage of.................per cent., on the c. f. & i. price, contract cancelled or not cancelled.

Buyer and Seller agree that, for the purpose of proceedings, either legal, or by arbitration, this contract shall
be deemed to have been made in England, to be performed there, any correspondence in reference to the offer,
the acceptance, the place of payment or otherwise notwithstanding, and the Courts of England or Arbitrators
appointed in England, as the case may be, shall, except for the purpose of enforcing any award made in
pursuance of the Arbitration clause hereof, have exclusive jurisdiction over all disputes which may arise
under this contract. Such disputes shall be settled according to the law of England whatever the domicile of
the parties to this contract may be or become. Any party to this contract residing in a foreign country,
shall, for the purpose of proceedings, be considered as residing at the Consulate in London of the country of
his residence. Any party to this Contract residing either in Scotland or Ireland, shall for the purpose of such
proceedings, be considered as residing at the offices of the London Corn Trade Association, and the service of
proceedings, as to the party residing in a foreign country at such Consulate, and the posting of a copy of
such proceedings to the address abroad of the party in question, and the service of proceedings, as to the
party residing in Scotland or Ireland, at the offices of the London Corn Trade Association, and the posting
of a copy of such proceedings to the address in Scotland or Ireland of the party in question, shall be deemed
good service, any rule of law to the contrary notwithstanding.

Difference in quality shall not entitle the Buyer to reject, except under the award of Arbitrators or the
Committee of Appeal, as the case may be. All disputes from time to time arising out of this contract,
whether arising between the parties hereto, or between one of the parties hereto and the Trustee in
Bankruptcy of the other party, shall be referred according to the Rule endorsed on this contract, and this
stipulation may be made a rule of any of the Divisions of Her Majesty's High Court of Justice in England
or in Ireland, or an order of the Court of Session in Scotland, on the application of either contracting party,
and neither Buyer, Seller nor Trustee in Bankruptcy, nor any other person claiming under either of them,
shall bring any action against the other of them in respect of any such dispute until such dispute has been
settled by Arbitration, or by the Committee of Appeal, as the case may be, and it is expressly agreed that the
obtaining an award from either tribunal, as the case may be, shall be a condition precedent to the right of
either contracting party to sue the other in respect of any claim arising out of this contract.

John Ross
President of the London Corn Trade Association, 1878–80

writers; that was the principle behind such contracts. The shipper took the risk in shipping; it was all part of his trade.

Mr Valieri failed to carry his fellow members and his amendment was lost by a majority of one. In view of the narrow margin it was agreed to try out the clause for twelve months and then review the situation. Valieri and his fellow Greek E. A. Mavrogordato came to the meeting with the intention of not allowing their names to go forward for re-election to the Committee, but in the event they relented. They were elected along with Messrs Aste, Usborne, Ross and Sechiari.

John Ross, who took the chair, said members were already aware that the London Corn Trade Association had offices and staff. In fact Edward Power was allowing them to use part of his office building rent free. But, said Ross, 'there is now every facility for carrying into effect all the objects for which the Association was formed'. The most perplexing problem was always the satisfactory settlement of what was fair average quality at the time and place of shipment. There was no more important object than forming authoritative standards for the use of arbitration. They had not yet had time to turn their attentions to charter-parties, bills of lading and insurance policies, but they would do so as soon as possible. Members heard that the President of the San Francisco Produce Exchange had presented the association with the 'standard samples' of shipping grades which they recognized.

By the time they met for their second annual meeting on 11 May 1880 15000 contract forms had been sold for the Black Sea Contract. 'The once little baby has commenced to walk,' said the honorary secretary John Kressman with justifiable pride, 'and I need not say how pleased its nurse is.' The East Indian wheat standard samples were being of great value to arbitrators. Standards now represented the whole of the shipments of Calcutta wheat to London. They had also established standards for no. 2 Red Winter, no. 2 North Western and nos. 2 and 3 Northern Spring.

Sea-damaged wheat was still a bone of contention, and Stephen Ralli held that a committee consisting of one buyer, one seller and one factor should decide the market price of wheat on certain days with reference to sea-damaged grain. Though arbitration played a key part in the smooth operation of the corn trade, not everyone was entirely happy with the way it worked. Mavrogordato thought the gentlemen chosen as arbitrators might err and there should be power of appeal to a higher court. But Edward Power, who had been one of the small group who helped found the LCTA, said if they had kept in the clause giving a right of appeal from the decisions of arbitrators they would never have been able to form the association, since it had met with great opposition.

The association had so much work on its hands it had to take additional offices at 22 Leadenhall Street, in addition to the room it had at Edward Power's building. John Kressman was ill and had sent the message expressing the pleasure of the 'nurse' in a written note. J. F. H. Woodward was acting for him as Secretary.

The association's reputation for fairness and efficiency soon spread to the continent, and in 1881 European firms asked it to appoint arbitrators in dispute between themselves and firms in the USA. The belief that arbitrators' first thoughts were best and should not be tampered with prevailed when the association's Executive Committee declined to form their own Appeal Committee to review decisions made by arbitrators – though only by a small majority.

Equal headway was being made in the adoption of forms of contract. They drafted one for the trade in Egyptian beans, and in the early part of 1881 they held talks with Liverpool over contracts for trade in Californian wheat. The Chambers of Commerce of Paris and Marseilles applied for portions of the standard samples adopted by the LCTA.

But in the 1880s there was by no means always unanimity among the Greeks and English on how the association should proceed. In 1884 the Executive Committee negatived a resolution that 'considering that one of the main objects of the association is to ensure uniformity of contracts and that it is not yet fully carried out by the trade, and to arrive at the desired conclusion, the Committee resolve that in future it will only take action on forms of contract made or approved by itself'. The votes were four for and six against. In April 1884 Edward Power had to withdraw his resolution to introduce new methods of arbitration and appoint a General Arbitration Committee composed of members of the LCTA who would be balloted for, from which a Sub-Committee would be formed to appoint and nominate arbitrators from the General Arbitration Committee.

Steam navigation was posing new problems and in 1884 the Executive Committee of the LCTA agreed at the request of Francis Lenders & Co, who queried Black Sea contracts, to enquire of the Secretary of Lloyds the proper definition of 'a first class steamer for grain'. They asked Mr Lenders himself to draft a clause which he considered met the new circumstances of transportation by steamship. Their views were sought by the Steam Ship Owners Mutual Protection and Indemnity Association. A member of the LCTA sat on the London Chamber of Commerce's Bills of Lading Committee. The association anxiously watched the passage through parliament of the Merchant Shipping Bill in the hope that it would result in a more just bill of lading to the benefit not only of the grain trade but other trades generally. With Lloyds they sought to mitigate the ill effect of every port in Europe having a different corn measure. They looked to the Merchant Shipping Bill to produce a clear definition of the word 'charterer' and sent a deputation to Joseph Chamberlain, the President of the Board of Trade, to express their views on what that should be.

In 1884 they printed and issued St Petersburg and Baltic Wheat Contracts and entered on long discussions about Australian, Chilean and Californian contracts. They had received standards of Californian and South Australian wheat but had not been successful in getting samples from United States ports.

They told the General Shipowners Society that a negligence clause in charter-parties and bills of lading would be favourably received by the corn trade, but they were not as happy about the Society's suggestion that in view of the general tendency towards cash payments in all departments of business they should support the efforts of shipowners to have all grain sailing ship freights paid in cash.

The LCTA's view was that this solely concerned the ship-owner and shipper, and was nothing to do with the receivers of cargoes in Britain. They did not feel called on to consent or dissent 'as any discount on freight in the new contract is to belong to the seller who is virtually the Shipper'. Nor were they prepared to subscribe to a fund for contesting the Railway Bills then before parliament. They had a strict sense of their *raison d'être* and would not allow themselves to become involved in contentious activities which were no business of theirs as an association, what-ever their private views might be.

What constituted 'negligence' however was of vital concern to the corn trade and it was something which had to be defined as closely as possible – and in terms both of steam navigation with its more complicated means of propulsion, and sail. For the latter the phrase 'or by improper opening of valves, sluices and ports' was omitted for instance; and for the former the word 'machinery' was substituted for 'masts, sails and rigging'. General agreement was reached that the negligence clause should read:

> The Act of God, Perils of the Sea, Fire, Barratry of the Master and Crew, Enemies, Pirates and Robbers, Arrests and Restraints of Princes, Rulers and People and other Accidents of Navigation excepted, Strandings and Collisions, and all Losses and Damages caused thereby are also excepted even when occasioned by negligence, default or error in judgement of the Pilot, Master, Mariners or other servants of the shipowners. . . .

But the shipowner was not exempt from liability for damage to cargo occasioned by bad stowage, improper drainage or ventilation, or defects in sails, provided they did not result from the want of diligence of the owners or ship's Husband or Manager.

Should a shipper be allowed – in the contract – to ship above or below a certain percentage of the quantity ordered without penalty? Should this margin be five or ten per cent? The LCTA Executive Committee in 1885 decided that a seller had the right to ship, by virtue of his contract, not exceeding five per cent above the maximum or below the minimum.

By 1886 the LCTA's activities had multiplied to such an extent that they could no longer operate in borrowed offices, and

Richard Duck was instructed to find suitable premises at a rent of not more than £60 a year. He found them at no. 2 Lime Street Square, and it was here that they held the meeting at which it was decided to incorporate the association. Articles of Association were drawn up which stated that the objects of the LCTA were

to promote and establish in the Corn Trade uniformity in commercial transactions and usages founded upon just and equitable principles, especially in regard to contracts, charter parties, bills of lading and policies of insurance; and to settle, circulate and promote the adoption of equitable and convenient forms of contract; to encourage settlement of disputes by arbitration; to collect samples to act as standards in arbitration; to institute or oppose legislation affecting people in the Corn Trade, and protect the interests of the Corn Trade, specially in London.

The subscribers to the memorandum were John Ross; Edward Majolier, corn factor; Richard Reid, corn factor; Samuel W. Keene, corn factor; Seth Taylor, miller; John H. Tod, merchant; R. J. Duck, corn factor. Marmaduke Cradock was Secretary.

That same year (1886) a society was formed called 'The Cereals' to promote social intercourse among members of the Grain and Allied Trades and their friends. The subscription was five shillings a year. Fourteen corn merchants joined in January and by June membership had jumped to forty-four. They held monthly dinners and they handed the proceeds of the first smoking concert (£20) to the Corn Exchange Benevolent Society.

Achieving uniformity of contract was once more a central purpose of the incorporated association, and its success in this regard was early established. The LCTA exerted considerable influence on the development of these contract forms whose flaws were exposed by the disputes which were brought to arbitration and revised in the light of decisions made by the arbitrators which the association appointed, and by judgements of the Court of Appeal and House of Lords. Two such judgements are outstanding as regards their effect on the interpretation and wording of LCTA contracts. When the Court of Appeal interpreted the word 'given' in the Appropriation Clause of a disputed contract for ss *Marigo L* as 'cause to be received', all contracts were amended accordingly. In the case of ss *Indianic* relating to a cargo of Australian wheat, the seller failed to tender the documents, and the House of Lords ruled that the original seller should pay his buyer the difference between the price at which the buyer had bought and the price at which he had re-sold the cargo, together with an indemnity for damages and costs which the buyer would have to pay to the buyer to whom the cargo had been re-sold. This judgement also led to contract forms being amended.

The international use of the Association's forms of contracts steadily expanded so that eventually, as a Grain Commission established by the Canadian Government reported, 'the major portion of the world's grain business is done upon the LCTA forms'.

A fundamental provision in every LCTA form of contract as seen, was that any dispute arising should be referred to arbitration in London, each party appointing one arbitrator and such arbitra-

Rules of the Cereals Society, 1886

tors having power to appoint an umpire if and when they disagreed.

The procedure was to be governed by the Arbitration Acts in
force at the time. If either party was dissatisfied with the arbitration award, although the principle was rejected in the early years,
right of appeal was later granted to a specially elected Board of
Appeal, subject to certain conditions being complied with by the
appellant. There was no appeal against awards for condition
where goods were sold on terms 'guaranteed sound on arrival
and/or Rye Terms' (a term that originally referred to shipments
of rye from Baltic ports).

If either of the parties so requested, where a point of law arose
in the course of the reference, the award could be stated in the
form of a Special Case for the decision of the high court. Over
the years such Special Cases were comparatively few in number.

As if to confirm the trade's preference for arbitration over litigation, the then Lord Chief Justice, in proposing the health of LCTA at its fiftieth anniversary dinner in 1928, said that he found himself in the curious position of proposing the health of the opposition.

Maintenance of the quality contracted for was as much their concern as ensuring just decisions in disputes. The LCTA instituted a procedure for dealing with complaints by receivers about the quality of commodities bought on 'certificate final' terms, by appointing superintendents to draw independent samples and to submit these to appointed experts for an examination and report. If the report supported the receiver's complaint, it was submitted to the authority concerned. In some cases an *ex gratia* payment was also obtained.

In 1887 the association issued Rules for the Sampling of Barley in Bulk because 'disputes have arisen between buyers and sellers of barley in bulk as to the proper method of taking samples of such cargoes for arbitration or analysis'. Samples, they said, should in future be taken jointly by buyer and seller at the port of discharge and sent to the LCTA whose property they became. One sample should be taken in every 100 buckets or sacks by the buyer and seller, each using a metal scoop of equal size from a sack in the hold or on deck.

And what should happen if the buyer of a cargo of grain for future delivery went bankrupt before he was able to take it? As it was, if the market went up the trustee of the bankrupt asked to have the goods delivered to him so he could sell at a profit, for the contract could not be cancelled. If the price went down the seller's loss was increased; he only had a right to claim against the estate and receive a dividend. The association recommended that if a buyer went bankrupt the seller should be entitled to consider the contract ended unless the bankrupt or his friends volunteered to honour it.

The authority which the LCTA had established as arbitrators in corn trade disputes, which was only the voluntary activity of a voluntary association however, though gratifying led to an assumption in 1888 which was hardly welcome. When in their discretion the LCTA declined to appoint arbitrators to settle a dispute, without giving any reason for their refusal, the solicitors of the firm against whom the complaint had been made claimed the refusal was tantamount to making an award against his client.

We would venture to point out to the Committee of the LCTA that by so doing the Committee would practically take upon themselves the position of arbitrators, as by refusing to appoint them they attempt to decide the question in dispute and put our clients in the same position as if an award had been made against them.

It was 'the duty' of the Committee to appoint arbitrators; though of course in using that word they were not expressing their view as to the obligations of the Committee under the contract. Seth Taylor, the president of the LCTA, took counsel's opinion which was that the association should take no further action.

There was no doubt about the popularity of this important LCTA service. In the twelve months May 1888 to April 1889 the association's Appeal Committee dealt with ninety-four cases, an increase of forty-three over the previous year – almost double.

When in 1888 Spillers the millers expressed concern about the application of the Merchandise Marks Act to sacks marked with the names of British corn merchants into which grain from overseas was emptied from a ship's hold, the LCTA wrote to the President of the Board of Trade asking him to receive a deputation to discuss the matter with a view to having the Act rescinded in this regard.

The development of the corn trade had always been influenced by communications, and at the end of the 1880s a new invention appeared to complement the electric telegraph, which in its day had revolutionized the making of transactions and the fixing of prices, particularly futures. This was the telephone, and at their meeting on 27 November 1888 'the chairman notified the Committee that the United Telephone Company would be willing to supply a direct wire from the offices of the association to the "Baltic" at the rate of £13 17s 6d per annum. E. Majolier proposed the offer be accepted if the Baltic Company gave sanction.' The arrangements were made before the year was out.

TELEPHONE Nº 4070.

London Corn Trade Association,

2, Lime Street Square,

London, E.C. 30 July 1890

To the Chairman of the
Baltic Committee,
South Sea House E.C.

Dear Sir,

In consequence of the Attendant to the Telephone instruments being away I would respectfully draw your attention to the fact that our direct wire is of no use whatever, inasmuch as the person placed there to look after same has not the slightest knowledge as to its working.

Yours faithfully,
R. J. Cradock
Secy.

31 July

In answer to yr. favor of yesterday I beg to inform you that our Telephone instruments were on that day under the charge of an operator from the head Telephone office who will remain till the return of our regular attendant. Regretting that there should have been any interruption &c &c

Letter to the Chairman of the Baltic Committee from the secretary of the London Corn Trade Association concerning the telephone service, 30 July 1890

FACING PAGE: *London Corn Trade Association, forms of contract in force, 1888*

London Corn Trade Association,

2, LIME STREET SQUARE,
LONDON, E.C.

M. J. CRADOCK, SECRETARY.

1888.

FORMS OF CONTRACTS IN FORCE.

1.— EAST INDIAN,		No. 1 Cargoes or Parcels (London Terms).
2.—	,,	No. 2 Cargoes or Parcels (Indian Terms).
3.—AUSTRALIAN,		No. 1 Cargoes (For Orders).
4.—	,,	No. 2 Parcels (Direct Port).
5.—CALIFORNIAN,		No. 1 Cargoes (For Shipment, Prompt unexpired).
6.—	,,	No. 2 Cargoes (Prompt, Expired or Arrived).
7.—	,,	No. 3 Parcels (Direct Port).
8.—CHILIAN,		Cargoes or Parcels.
9.—AMERICAN,		No. 1 Cargoes (For Orders).
10.—	,,	No 2 Parcels (Direct Port).
11.—LA PLATA,		No. 1 Cargoes (For Orders, *tale quale*).
12.—	,,	No. 2 Parcels (Direct Port, *tale quale*).
13.—	,,	No. 3 Cargoes (For Orders, Rye Terms).
14.—	,,	No. 4 Parcels (Direct Port, Rye Terms).
15.—EGYPTIAN,		Bean and Lentil ($7\frac{1}{2}$ per cent, dirt clause.)
16.—BLACK SEA AND DANUBIAN,		No. 1 Cargoes (For Orders, for Shipment, *tale quale*).
17.—	,, ,,	No. 1 Parcels (Direct Port, ,, ,,).
18.—	,, ,,	No. 2 Cargoes (For Orders, on Passage, ,,).
19.—	,, ,,	No. 2 Parcels (Direct Port, ,, ,,).
20.—	,, ,,	No. 3 Cargoes (For Orders, Arrived, ,,).
21.—	,, ,,	No. 4 Cargoes (For Orders, for Shipment, S/D).
22.—	,, ,,	No. 4 Parcels (Direct Port, ,, ,,).
23.—	,, ,,	No. 5 Cargoes (For Orders, on Passage ,,).
24.—	,, ,,	No. 5 Parcels (Direct Port, ,, ,,).
25.—	,, ,,	No. 6 Cargoes (For Orders, Arrived, ,,).
26.—	,, ,,	No. 7 Cargoes (For Orders, for Shipment, Rye Terms).
27.—	,, ,,	No. 7 Parcels (Direct Port, ,, ,,).
28.—	,, ,,	No. 8 Cargoes (For Orders on Passage, ,,).
29.—ST. PETERSBURG & BALTIC,		No. 1 Cargoes (For Orders, for Shipment, S/D).
30.—	,, ,,	No. 2 Parcels or Cargoes (London Direct, for Shipment, S/D.)
31.—RULES FOR SAMPLING BARLEY IN BULK.		

N.B.—The above Forms of Contracts are registered at Stationers' Hall. Members and others are cautioned against any infringement of copyright.

BOOK OF CONTRACTS.

Price to Members	....	3s. 0d.
,, Non-Members	....	6s. 0d.

The wire would certainly have been kept busy, for in 1888 the LCTA had thirty forms of contract in force – see the list reproduced on page 33. There were two East Indian, two Australian, three Californian, one Chilean, two American, four for La Plata, one Egyptian, thirteen Black Sea and Danubian, two St Petersburg and Baltic.

When corn merchants on the River Plate planned to introduce a system of grain inspection, William Goodwin a member of the LCTA, hurried out to South America to give them advice – and see no doubt that it was not going to be over-restrictive. Lenders & Co suggested putting in a clause in the La Plata contract forms that the seller had an option of shipping by steamers at liberty to discharge cargo at one or more ports in the UK or on the continent before delivering goods tendered in the contract.

It was one thing to draw up contracts, another to get firms to complete them. Because of the difficulty of the latter, many Antwerp banks gave notice that they would pay or accept only against full sets of bills of lading for shipments of grain. Banks in France made similar stipulations. Many sellers in London were objecting to delivering all copies of bills of lading, Francis Lenders told the LCTA Committee, so that the London contract must provide that buyers should pay against one copy, accompanied maybe by a letter of guarantee from the seller.

Some of the earliest contracts of the LCTA had clauses that specified the maximum amount of 'admixture' in parcels of grain and seed, with allowances if these limits were exceeded. Allowances of this nature could make all the difference between a profit and a loss on the transaction, and it was apparent that the association needed the services of an analyst of integrity capable of determining the percentage of admixture for the purpose of these contracts. So in 1888 the association appointed Dr Bernard S. Dyer official analyst.

Dyer had received his early training in agricultural chemistry as a pupil-assistant in the laboratory of Dr Augustus Voelcker, consulting chemist to the Royal Agricultural Society. When he was only twenty-one Dyer had his own laboratory at 17 Great Tower Street, London, and quickly acquired a reputation as an agricultural analyst following the investigations he carried out in conjunction with Rothampstead Experimental Station in the field of soil analysis.

In determining the percentage of admixture in samples of grain submitted to the LCTA, he admitted that at first his analyses were subject to 'experimental error' – he had not appreciated the difficulties involved in taking a fair sample from bulk. But he quickly realized that since in all LCTA contracts the analyst's certificate was final – there was no provision for a second analysis – he had to eliminate any possible error that might arise from inadequate sampling. He certainly succeeded, for in almost every case today the analyst's certificate is final.

The wording of grain contracts and charter parties was continually evolving to match the changing commercial and social climate. Corn merchants from Liverpool, Hull and the West of England attended a meeting in January 1890 to debate whether a 'strike clause' should be inserted. They passed a resolution that it was most desirable that one should be put into all charter parties. Uniformity was still far from total at the end of the nineteenth century, and vaguely worded contracts were still in operation chartering steamers or sailing ships, for instance, to discharge 'as fast as ships can deliver' or 'according to the custom of the port'. This led to time-consuming disputes and annoyances, said the Bristol Channel and West of England Corn Trade Association, who asked for the LCTA's opinion in 1891. The London association said their view was that charters in the grain trade should specify a certain number of lay days for discharge, and declared they would consult with the General Shipowners Society about having such a clause put in all charter parties. But when later that year the UK Chamber of Shipping announced they were trying to arrange a conference to consider revising the present scale of lay days in grain charters from America, the LCTA said this was not its concern 'as it is a question entirely between shipowners and charterers'.

A similar sense of minding its own business led the LCTA to refuse an application from the London Chamber of Commerce in 1892 to nominate a member to the Chamber's Bills of Lading Committee on the grounds that mutual bills of lading were agreed between the LCTA and shipowners.

Liaison with the Liverpool body had always been strong, but it does not seem to have been enhanced by the new means of communication in the way the promoters of the telephone service had promised. On 18 December 1896 A. B. Gripper, secretary of the LCTA, received the following letter from Jno. McGuirk, assistant secretary of the Liverpool Corn Trade Association.

A. B. Gripper Esq.
Secretary, London Corn Trade Association.

Dear Sir,
    Complaints of the inadequacy of the present Trunk Line Service between Liverpool and London having been laid before my Directors, a deputation from their body waited upon the Liverpool Postmaster with a view to obtaining improved telephonic and telegraphic facilities, and, if possible, to induce the Post Office to provide a separate wire for each service for the exclusive use of the Corn Trade.
    It has been suggested that the co-operation of your Association would greatly assist in bringing about better communication between the two markets, and I am to point out to you that when the trunk telephone was first opened it was found to be of great service, connection could be made with London and a conversation completed within a few minutes time. Now, connection is rarely made within an hour, and sometimes it takes nearly an hour and a half. Telegraphic communication is equally defective. I need not remind you that the valuable time which is too frequently consumed waiting for replies to telegrams or for telephonic connection seriously militates against the interests of both Associations.

    What appears to be wanted is:—
(1). A direct telephone wire between the Baltic in London and the Atlantic in Liverpool, with a Post Office box (not a Company's box) in each place.
(2). A direct telegraph wire between the Baltic P.O. London and the Corn Exchange P.O. Liverpool.

    I am instructed to ask your Association to kindly take this matter up and to approach the Postmaster General on the lines I have indicated. Similar representations are being made to the authorities here.
    Hoping to receive a favourable reply,

        I am,
            Yours faithfully,
                (Signed) Jno. McGuirk, Asst. Secretary.

TELEPHONE Nº 4070.

TELEGRAPHIC ADDRESS,
"CONSIGNMENT, LONDON."

London Corn Trade Association,

2 Lime Street Square,

London, E.C.   Dec. 23rd, 1896.

c o p y.

The Secretary,

       Liverpool Corn Trade Association.

Dear Sir,

       re Direct Telephone & Telegraphic Wires between the Baltic in

           London & the Atlantic in Liverpool.

       Your letter of the 18th inst. re above was before my Executive
Committee yesterday, who instruct me to inform you that the "Baltic" Company has approached the Post Office in reference to a direct Telegraph wire
from the Baltic to the Corn Exchange Liverpool. And my Committee considers
it would be better for the Baltic Company to communicate with the Post
Office in reference to a direct Telephone wire.

       I am therefore instructed to write to the Baltic Company on the
matter.

              Yours faithfully,

                (Signed) A.B.Gripper,

                    Secretary.

*Letter from the Secretary of the London Corn Trade Association, concerning a
direct telephone wire, 23 December 1896*

Troubles over the sending of messages were secondary to those over the sending across very much larger distances the commodity which was the subject of these telephone communications. In 1899 the amount of 'dirt and foreign substance' which continued to be included in shipments of grain from Russia and India was causing concern not only to corn merchants but, even more, to their customers the millers. At a meeting in December 1899 with the National Association of British and Irish Millers (which incidentally had been formed in the same year as the LCTA, 1878) the LCTA told the millers' representatives that shippers were unwilling to insert clauses specifying dirt limits in contracts. There had been talk of restricting acceptable impurities to one, two or three per cent of the bulk. NABIM then asked if a sealed sample on which the sale was based could be analysed, and the analysis taken into account in cases where there was arbitration. At a general meeting in Sheffield that April the millers' association resolved to approach the Board of Trade and the India Office to bring their attention to the practice of adulterating wheat for shipment to Britain.

By the time the new century had dawned and Queen Victoria had breathed her last (in January 1901), the London Corn Trade Association had established itself as an essential component of Britain's commercial life and a body to which the many complicated problems relating to the international grain trade were automatically referred not only by those who traded in Britain which was its centre, but by traders in every corner of the world.

2

The changing pattern of the twentieth-century corn trade fathers the LCFTA, the LGFA – and the Depression
1900–1938

When the London Shipping Exchange and 'The Baltic' merged to form The Baltic Mercantile and Shipping Exchange they moved from their respective premises at Billiter Street and South Sea House into the new headquarters they built for themselves in St Mary Axe off Leadenhall Street, which was opened by the Lord Mayor of London in April 1903. Apart from the exchange's floor and restaurants, the building contained a number of office suites – 'Baltic Chambers' – and it was into one of these on the fourth floor that the London Corn Trade Association moved as a tenant.

Three years later a number of members of the LCTA who traded in the vegetable proteins, which were just being introduced to the market, decided that their activities were of so specialist a nature and so different from the run-of-the-mill corn trade that they warranted separate handling, particularly as regards arbitration. For the most part these were Importing Wholesale Dealers, and on 28 August 1906 a leading operator in this field, Herbert Grimsdale, chaired a meeting in the Board Room of the Corn Exchange in Mark Lane at which a resolution was passed that 'an Association be formed of Sellers and Buyers of all descriptions of Cakes and Feeding Stuffs to endeavour to establish uniform contracts, a system of arbitration, and to promote the interests of

FOLLOWING THREE PAGES: *The first minute of the London Cattle Food Trade Association, concerning the formation of the Association, 1906*

1

28th. August, 1906.

Minutes of a meeting held at the Board Room of the Corn Exchange Co., Mark Lane, on the 28th. August, 1906, by kind permission of the Board; Mr. D. Herbert Grimsdale in the Chair; the following Firms being present who all promised to join the Association:- Messrs. T. J. Pemberton & Co., R. J. Hewetson, John Burstall & Co., E. A. White & Co., J. A. Anderson & Co., Walker Winser & Ham, Pinnock Bros., Neville, Green & Fowler, O'Brien Butcher, Ltd., Cook & Mason & Co., Anderson, Fairley, Brown, Cubitt & Son, The Copland, Raymond, Leon, Co., Cornwell, Son & Heath, Grimsdale Bros., Hamlyn & Co. Ltd. also present, Mr. Worrall.

D.H.G.

The Chairman stated that it had been mooted that it was advisable that for the benefit of the Cake & Meal Trade, an Association should be formed in the interest of Buyers & Sellers & moved the following resolution, which, after a general discussion was seconded by Mr. R. R. Green & carried unanimously:-

1. That an association be formed of Sellers & Buyers of all descriptions of Cakes & Feeding Stuffs to endeavour to establish uniform Contracts; a system of Arbitration & to promote the interests of

the Trade generally.

2. Proposed by the Chairman & seconded by Mr W. H. Pinnock & carried "That the name of the Association be "The London Cattle Food Trade Association".

3. Proposed by the Chairman & seconded by Mr Thompson & carried "That the subscription be £2.2.0 per annum".

4. Proposed by the Chairman & seconded by Mr Neville & carried "That the business of the Association be conducted by an Executive Committee of fourteen, to consist of the President, Vice-President, Treasurer, Hon. Secretary & ten Members who shall as far as possible, represent, both Buyers & Sellers in the various Trades interested.

5. Proposed by the Chairman & seconded by Mr Butcher & carried "That the first Committee be now elected to remain in office until the first General Meeting "that they be requested to draw up Rules and Regulations to be submitted to a General Meeting of the Association.

It was agreed to ask Mr Fred. Gossard to act as President & he was elected, being seconded by Mr Newetson.

The Vice Presidentship was accepted Mr D. R. Trinsdale being proposed by Mr Pinnock, seconded by Mr Green.

The Treasurership was accepted by Mr Ward being seconded by Mr Pinnock.

The Honorary Secretaryship was accepted by Mr H. C. Hamlyn being seconded by Mr Ward.

The following gentlemen were duly elected on the Executive Committee & promised to stand:- Mr W. Pinnock. Mr R R Green, Mr Douglas Cubitt, Mr E t White, Mr Wm Hewetson, & Mr M. A Toomey.

It was agreed to ask the following Gentlemen to join the Committee: Mr Mason (failing him Mr Bawcomb) Mr Arthur Todd, Mr Scott (or Mr T C Ward & Mr Gordon, failing these Mr Marcus, Mr R Herne Mr Payne or Mr Drakeford.

Letters were received from the following approving of the Association who recommended the Sack question to be gone into, Messrs Blott Long & Co, Geo Snelling, Shipton Anderson & C, & Chatterton & Co.

The Meeting closed with a vote of thanks to the Chairman.

S. H. Grimsdale

18/9/06.

the Trade generally'. The Association was to be called 'The London Cattle Food Trade Association'. The original objects of the Association were:

To establish in the Cattle Food* Trade, uniformity in commercial usages, especially with regard to contracts, charter parties, bills of lading, policies of insurance, and to appoint official analysts, and to make such use of their services as may be thought desirable in the interests of the trade; to settle and circulate equitable and convenient forms of contract and any other documents which may be of use to the trade; to encourage the settlement of disputes by arbitration, and to appoint arbitrators and umpires for the settlement of such disputes, and to constitute a court of appeal. To receive or take samples to serve as standards for arbitration; to provide, when necessary, suitable premises where standard samples may be kept and arbitrations held; to institute, promote, support, or oppose legislative or other measures or proceedings affecting the interests of the members of the trade; to introduce any reforms and undertake any arrangements which from time to time may commend themselves to the Executive Committee.

While the initiative to form the association was taken by the Importing Wholesale Dealers, membership was not restricted. Very soon all sections of the trade were represented in its membership, including overseas firms, thus the association became international in character.

The new association had its own offices at 8 Catherine Street, EC, which it rented for £50 a year. It was governed by an elected Council which included similar officers to the LCTA as well as *ex officio* representatives of Section Committees and representatives of the main port associations. In 1909 it held its first annual dinner, and in 1912 moved to 50 Mark Lane.

When war came in 1914 the government undertook to guarantee war risks on wheat and flour shipped, and to be shipped, from Canadian and Atlantic ports to the UK under existing contracts. The Kaiser's submarine blockade of Britain seriously threatened her food supplies which demanded drastic measures outside the scope of private enterprise geared to normal trading conditions. But there were many who resented government 'interference', and many members of the LCTA and The Baltic made strong

---

* Nowadays the word 'feed' is normally used for anything intended to be fed to animals, as in the association's present title The Grain and Feed Trade Association.

SALE OF GRAIN BY WEIGHT,
WITH UNIFORMITY.

Great inconvenience, with delay and increase of cost, arises from the present inaccurate method of selling Grain by various Weights and Measures throughout the kingdom.

The system of selling Grain by Measure is universally admitted as inaccurate, and in many Markets selling by Weight (*in some form*) has been substituted.

The object now desired, is to establish the sale of Grain by WEIGHT, with UNIFORMITY.

In making the change, injury and inconvenience should be avoided, to Shipowners as carriers; the Customs, as Collectors of Duty; and to Importers, as Contractors for purchase and sale; also, to create as little disturbance as possible in the present forms of contracts, in which great advantages will arise in preserving the name of the IMPERIAL QUARTER, so universally known abroad and at home as the British Standard.

To gain these objects, it is proposed to form a Deputation to wait on the Secretary of the Board of Trade, requesting that a short Act of Parliament may be passed establishing hereafter the Imperial Bushel of Grain, as,

40 lbs. of OATS,

50 lbs. of BARLEY,

60 lbs. of WHEAT,

Other Grain, in proportion, to be arranged with equitable care.

If adopted, the Customs would then collect Duty *by weight*. Freight would be paid by *weight;* and considering that Twelve Millions of Quarters are annually imported into the various Markets of the Kingdom, *Uniformity* in the sale by *weight* promises success, and the honest Trader would be better protected from frauds and disputes, at present of daily occurrence.

Statistic Returns of Agricultural Produce and of Foreign Imports would be more accurate, and more easily collected.

If approved, when signed, please forward this to

THE SECRETARY,

COMMITTEE OF MERCHANTS,

BALTIC COFFEE-HOUSE,

LONDON.

WE, the undersigned, Importers, Shipowners, Corn Factors, and Merchants of _Gloster_ , do respectfully request that the Right Honorable the Secretary to the Board of Trade will take the above sought for changes into his favorable consideration, and thus increase the facilities in the Sale and Import of Grain, forming so important a Branch in the Trade and Commerce of the United Kingdom :—

J. M. Sturge, Commercial Agent.

J W Kimberly — Merchant Gloster

Hy Adams & Merchants &

Josiah James & Co Merchants Gloucester

Vining & Co Merchants Gloucester

M Cerry & Co Do Do

W C Rowley & Son Do Do

John Robinson Do Do

Reynolds & Allen Do Do

Proposal for the sale of grain by weight submitted to the Board of Trade

representations to the Board of Agriculture and Fisheries about the bulk purchase of wheat as 'security reserves'. The government, perhaps necessarily in the circumstances, had not informed the trade of its intentions, and this had created uncertainty and a lowering of market prices. The LCTA's protest brought a letter from the Board of Agriculture promising that it would make no further purchases.

In July 1915 the LCTA notified the Baltic Exchange that certain American firms had given notice that they had revoked all agreements for arbitration contained in shipments of grain to ports in Norway, Sweden, Denmark, Holland, Belgium, France, Italy and Mediterranean Africa which had been entered into before August 1914. James Findlay, secretary of The Baltic,

posted the association's letter on the Floor of the exchange and
gave instructions that the 'waiters' on the door should refuse
entry to any representatives of these American firms in accordance
with the standing orders applicable to those who failed to carry
out their contracts.

Many prominent members of the corn trade served on the
Royal Commission on Wheat Supplies, which early in 1917 took
over on behalf of the government the control of all imports of
wheat and animal feeding stuffs. The functions of the LCTA and
LCFTA were virtually suspended, but the area committees of
both associations were made responsible for controlling the
distribution of imported feeding stuffs. Grain analysis continued
throughout the war, and when Dr Bernard Dyer, LCTA's
official analyst, formed his practice into a limited company, Dr
Bernard Dyer and Partners Limited, the firm became the association's official analysts in his place.

A principal customer of the Royal Commission on Wheat
Supplies was The Australian Wheat Committee in London. A
contract for a quantity of 'Australian Wheat old &/or new crop
at sellers option' – three million tons at 38s a quarter, dated 4
December 1916 was 'sold to the account of The Hon. W. M.
Hughes' who was the Prime Minister of Australia.

A typewritten attachment set out how each of the States of
Australia would get its due proportion of the 3 000 000 tons. Lay
days for steamers of 6000 tons deadweight were eight weather
working days at Sydney or Melbourne and ten at others, except
South Australia outports which had five days extra. 'Sailers' had
ten days. The Royal Commission agreed to pay extra charges in
the event of the grain not being shipped by 31 December 1917.
'It is further agreed that after 31st December 1917 all risks of
deterioration from natural causes affecting the quality and any
loss in weight due to weevil shall be account of The Royal
Commission on Wheat Supplies.' All vessels were acting under
instructions of the British Admiralty.

Following the formation of Corn Trade Associations in Liverpool,
Glasgow, and London, merchants in other ports had followed

The floor of the Baltic Exchange, circa 1916

their lead. The Hull Corn Trade Association with forty-two members was founded in March 1888 and registered under the Companies Act in 1896. At the end of the century they built themselves the Pacific Exchange. The Bristol Channel and West of England Corn Trade Association began life in 1889, the Leith Corn Trade Association in 1890. In 1918 these six formed the National Federation of Corn Trade Associations and invited three groups in the same field to join them – the National Association of Corn and Agricultural Merchants (NACAM), the National Association of British and Irish Millers (NABIM), and the Maltsters Association of Great Britain.

The Federation's objects (like those of many of its member associations) were primarily to represent and protect the interests of the trade as a whole. The most important of these, as set out in the memorandum of the association were:

To discuss and consider and deal with all questions concerning and affecting and relating to the Corn Trade and other trades connected or having relations or business with the Corn Trade or with which it may be to the advantage of the Federation and its members to have dealings or relations.

To discuss and consider and deal with all questions concerning government or state, county, municipal or other official control of the Corn Trade or of matters affecting or concerning the Corn Trade including in particular the control of agriculture, land carriage and shipping in the United Kingdom and abroad, and of exports and imports and distribution and to represent the Corn Trade in any discussion or negotiations with any government or state or any public or official body, either in the United Kingdom or abroad, and to conclude agreements, conventions and regulations in relation thereto.

To promote or oppose or join with any other person or body, corporate or unincorporate, in promoting or opposing legislative and other measures affecting or calculated to affect the Corn Trade and in particular to petition any Parliament, government or other bodies or persons as may be expedient and to appoint delegates to attend before commissions, committees, ministers or officials; and to prepare and present and co-operate with any other person or body in the preparation and presentation in Parliament of Bills affecting or in the interest of the Corn Trade and to procure the adequate representation thereof upon all committees or commissions whose terms of reference may affect or deal with the Corn Trade.

The Federation provided a most useful forum and became a well used channel of communication with government departments and other organizations.

When the war ended and the LCTA was able to resume its peacetime activities, it decided to bring its machinery up to date. In 1919 it set its Contracts Committee to revise the whole range of forms. Each contained some 5000 words and the task took two years.

In 1919 too the London Cattle Food Trade Association made arrangements with the London Oil and Tallow Trades Association for the use of office accommodation at 50 Lime Street, and the services of a Secretary and staff, for £225 a year. This was the forerunner of United Associations Limited, created in 1922 to rent and furnish offices for any trade association which required them.

The nominal capital of this service company was £5000 shared by the associations represented on its Board of Directors. A year later they moved to 84 Leadenhall Street.

In January 1922, the LCTA opened a clearing house through which contracts were registered and cash differences on them settled more particularly in respect of string transactions. The first commodities covered were Plate maize and Plate oats. The former was very actively traded and the record string contained well over one hundred transactions.

In 1925, contracts for Japanese green peas were accepted for registration and in 1926 contracts for Madagascar butter beans. The making up of Standards for quality arbitrations and the ascertainment of Natural Weight were two important services continued by the London Corn Trade Association at this time and in great demand by the trade.

The Corn Exchange in the 1920s, showing the old clock, the stands for samples and one of the waiters

1924 was the year of the British Empire Exhibition at Wembley and the LCFTA helped in organizing exhibits of various oil seeds for it. The exhibition demonstrated to the world how quickly Britain had recovered from the war. Britain was certainly once more the centre of the international grain trade, and this was reflected in the London Corn Trade Association's membership which included the 500 leading grain firms of the world, a third of which operated from headquarters outside Britain. Every day an average of 100 tons of grain samples were held at the association's store in the basement under Baltic Chambers for arbitration, standards, natural weights and the rest. In 1923 it had made 2000 arbitration awards. Every year it collected more than 6000 samples for making Fair Average Quality standards. Another 70000 were received for arbitrations. Every year it sold 320000 forms of contract. Stanley H. Titford had succeeded A. B. Gripper as secretary and he devoted much time to explaining the role of the association to the post-war generation of corn merchants, and educating them in the traditions which had given London its reputation for probity and fair dealing.

The problem of impurity and adulteration was as pressing in the post-war years as it had ever been before 1914, and the services of the association's analyst Dr Bernard Dyer were in great demand. To assess the percentage of admixture, the buyers' agent selected one original bag for every 100 tons, but of each mark not less than five and not more than sixty bags were chosen. The bags were placed in dust-proof covers made of sail-cloth canvas and sent to one of the LCTA's three reducing agents in London, the PLA, Greens or Cooks. At the premises of each of these was a reducing machine. On the top floor of the building was a hopper into which was emptied the contents of the bags. The grain fell to rotating circular sieves on the floor below which extracted bulky impurities like straw, husks and lumps of dirt which fell to a large tank on the next floor. It was then weighed, sealed, recorded and passed to the analyst.

On the ground floor was the reducing machine proper which, by means of a revolving fan-shaped apparatus, separated a one per cent sample, the other 99 per cent passing away down a chute to be re-sacked. The one per cent sample was sent to Dr Dyer, and from the 99 per cent residue sealed arbitration and standard samples, and open samples for the seller and buyer, were taken. Before the latter were bagged and sealed, they were passed over an automatic sieve of fine mesh in order to extract all remaining dust and dirt. The reducing agents also ascertained and recorded the tare of all the bags received. The residue of the grain was dealt with by the sellers to whom it belonged. On completion the LCTA issued an analysis certificate to the interested parties. In the 1920s, when this elaborate analysis and reducing procedure was the rule, the association charged from £3 3s for 100 tons to £18 18s for 5000 tons.

The association also undertook at this time to certify the 'natural weight' of Plate and other wheat, rye and oats which were sold with a warranty of the weight of a given cubic capacity measure. The seller sold on a guaranteed weight at the time of discharge. There was obviously a greater milling product from wheat weighing 62½ lb a bushel than from wheat weighing 60 lb a bushel. If the seller failed in shipping to his guarantee, he compensated the buyer by a percentage reduction of the contract price according to fixed scales. The method adopted by the LCTA in the 1920s was aimed at eliminating a rough-and-ready system in which the human element played too large a part for accuracy, and making the operation more scientific. For the weighing they installed a beam balance machine known as the Schopper Scale which measured in kilograms (to one gram) whereas the old McQuirk, or bushel weighing machine, registered to a quarter of an ounce. The Schopper Scale was seven times finer in measurement than McQuirk. The sample was weighed five times by a team of three men – a weigher and two check weighers – who each in turn independently took and recorded the weight of each twenty-litre load. Each weight had to tally before being passed through a Sommer and Runge one-litre scale as a further check. From a comparative scale they then computed pounds per bushel (or kilograms per hectolitre) and a certificate was made out. The fee for ascertaining Natural Weight was a guinea to five guineas according to quantity.

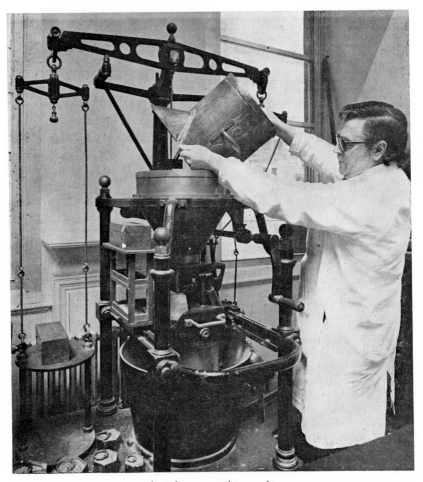

The Schopper weighing machine

In 1925 the London Cattle Food Trade Association appointed Mr M. Salamon to be their official analyst. He was then a partner in the analyst firms of both John Hughes and Salamon & Seaber. In 1947 the two firms separated and the appointment was given to Messrs Salamon & Seaber who are still the official analysts of GAFTA for proteins.

Nearly a thousand factors joined the Feedingstuffs Trade Benevolent Society when it was founded in 1924 with a funded capital of £60000 – a measure of the scale on which the Cattle Feeding Stuffs trade was now operating. The following year the

London Cattle Food Association was registered under the Companies Act as a company limited by guarantee and not having a share capital. The certificate of incorporation was dated 26 February 1925. It had 174 members. In 1923 the firm of John Hughes was appointed the association's official analyst. Mr M. Salamon was a partner in both John Hughes and Messrs Salamon & Seaber.

Both the LCTA and the LCFTA who had played so important a part in the evolution of arbitration gave evidence to the Committee which the Lord Chancellor set up in 1926, under the chairmanship of Mr Justice Mackinnon, to review the law and practice of arbitration. The most important of this committee's proposals was one that emphasized the need to expedite proceedings when an award was stated in the form of a Special Case for the decision of the High Court. Arbitration procedure at this time was governed by the Arbitration Act of 1886. The submission was to two arbitrators, one appointed by each party to the dispute, and these two could appoint a third. Their award was made on a form supplied by the LCTA who charged 10s for it if the parties were members, 20s if not. If one of the parties refused to appoint an arbitrator the LCTA contract stipulated that the LCTA could appoint one. There was a right of appeal to a tribunal consisting of five elected members of the Association's Appeal Committee.

Though all documents were passed, contracts settled and the clearing of differences facilitated through its Clearing House, the LCTA accepted no responsibility for fulfilment of a contract and in no way relieved parties' liability to each other. In another sense The Baltic Exchange also acted as a 'clearing house' for the cereal produce of the world in the 1920s, for its main function was organizing the movement of the crops from exporting countries to fulfil the requirements of the importers. The task involved the chartering of shipping under every flag and the financing in every currency of the millions of tons of grain in its movement to every quarter of the globe. Naturally enough both the LCTA and the LCFTA worked very closely with The Baltic and formed an important link in its world-wide activity.

Leading grain and oil seed brokers were pleased to co-operate when the chairman of The Baltic, Sir Ernest Glover, called a meeting at the exchange in March 1927 to discuss the role of the broker in the corn trade. H. A. Francis of Whitson, Nielson & Francis said for the last few years the trade had been tending in the direction of pools and combines, and he blamed the lack of co-operation among the grain brokers for their position in the trade. He did not think there could be any tangible improvement without the initiative being taken by the Federation of Corn Trade Associations. The directors of The Baltic could not force the trade to conduct its business in any particular way, but could help by insisting that its members complied with the rules and regulations laid down by the Corn Trade Associations. The London Corn Trade Association contract was paramount through-out Europe; it was a powerful weapon with which to force everyone to conform to those methods accepted by the majority in the trade as suiting best the common interest. Directly the Corn Associations formed any set of rules for trading the brokers would have to conform to them at the risk of expulsion from the Corn Trade Associations and The Baltic.

H. L. Routh of Payne and Routh (a future president of the LCTA) on the other hand, said the question of buying and selling through a broker had been discussed by the London Corn Trade Association for the past six months without their coming to any definite conclusion. The London Corn Trade Contract in his opinion was no longer paramount throughout the world, let alone on the continent. There was one contract at Hamburg, another at Antwerp and another at Rotterdam. The outcome of inserting fresh conditions in the London Corn Trade Contract would probably be to lose continental business. Drastic action by the Board of the Baltic Exchange would do more harm than good.

Francis returned to the debate to point out that three-quarters of the wheat sold by the Canadian Wheat Pool had to find a market in Britain and it should not be allowed to be sold except on Britain's terms put through the usual channels of the trade.

B. Woodward said when the Labour government were in power in 1924 they had prepared a comprehensive scheme for 'working' the grain and flour trades, and they would probably bring it out again if they were re-elected. In his opinion there should be a triple combination of millers, shippers and brokers to combat any government interference. The grain brokers were having a particularly bad time and London merchants should consider evolving a new speculative contract. No trade could exist without a certain amount of reasonable speculation. The Federation of Corn Trade Associations had already taken the matter up.

Richard Reid, a prime mover in the formation of the LCTA, was a member of the Grain Committee which The Baltic appointed to investigate the whole problem. The main circumstance which had promoted the changed status of the grain broker was the appearance of the big combinations of millers who, as Sir Arthur Holmes of Shipton, Anderson & Co. said, were threatening to freeze out those who had made the corn trade by placing bulk orders direct with the farmer/producers. He suggested that The Baltic, The Pacific and The Atlantic, together with the Corn Trade Associations in collaboration with the Federation, should withhold the rights and privileges of membership from millers who did not buy through the usual channels of the trade – either a corn merchant or a broker.

There was no doubt the corn trade had a crisis on its hands, and to meet it the National Federation of Corn Trade Associations appointed a Trade Re-organization Sub-Committee to prescribe a remedy. On 18 January 1928 it held a conference at which it passed three resolutions. The first was that the meeting was sympathetic to the ideas that efforts should be made to restore the corn trade to its normal conditions and that a small sub-committee should be appointed to confer and see how best to give effect to those wishes. The second was that this sub-committee should consist of merchants and brokers, the Corn Trade Federation and Associations, and the third that the chairman of the Federation should appoint the sub-committee's members. The chairman of this sub-committee was Henry Hosegood and it included Sir S. F. Mendl, MP, a leading member of the LCTA, and for some

London Corn Trade Association.

Telephones: Avenue 5146 (3 Lines).
Telegrams: Consignment, Stock, London.
Code: 5th Edition A.B.C.

Exchange Chambers,
28. St. Mary Axe,
London, E.C.3.

Ref.......................... ....

March 19th., 1929.

The Secretary,
Baltic Mercantile & Shipping Exchange,Ltd.,
E.C.3.

Dear Sir,

The Association proposes to establish, at an early date, a London C.I.F. Wheat Futures Market, and I am directed to ask if your Board will kindly grant facilities for setting up the necessary ring and price marking board on the floor of the Exchange.

The Association will be responsible for employing the ring attendants required for recording and marking the prices.

I enclose a copy of the draft regulations, which have been drawn up to govern trading in this Market.

The Association will be pleased to give your Board any further information which may be desired, either through its Chairman - Mr. H.L. Routh, Vice-Chairman - Sir Herbert Robson, or the undersigned.

Yours faithfully,

Cauley Hufard

Secretary.

L.D.   Enc.

time its honorary treasurer. They submitted their report on 27 March 1928 after examining every section of the corn trade in order to find a way out of their difficulties.

'We regret that after many hours of anxious thought and pains-taking endeavour we have found that, whilst a large measure of sympathy and support has been accorded to the principle em-bodied in Resolution 1, it is impossible to reach a general agree-ment.' They were of the opinion, however, that 'drastic proposals' must be adopted 'to remove the evils which have developed in the trade rather than depend upon partial measures which, although perhaps securing temporary relief, yet must inevitably lead to a recurrence of the existing trouble'. They suggested the corn trade should be divided into four classes – producers, mer-chants, brokers and consumers/millers; that members of each association should sign an undertaking in respect of the sale or purchase of all grain on CIF ex ship or landed terms to UK ports in accordance with the conditions of their particular classifi-cation. Producers should undertake not to enter into any contract with millers except through the medium of merchants or brokers. Three of the seven members of the sub-committee dissented, and the plan was quietly shelved *sine die*.

The faith which Mr Woodward had expressed in a small dose of speculation as a boost to an ailing trade bore fruit when in March 1929 the London Corn Trade Association established the London Grain Futures Association (incorporated on 3 May) under whose auspices the London Grain Futures Market was inaugurated on the floor of the Baltic Exchange, where it set up a 'ring' round which representatives of member firms gathered and traded by 'open outcry'. The basis of the market was Manitoba and Argen-tine wheat with a unit of 1000 quarters of 480 lb each on CIF terms. Trading took place twice a day between 11.30 a.m. and noon, and between 2.45 and 4.30. Each party to a sale deposited with the LCTA Clearing House an original margin of £50 on

---

A letter to the Secretary of the Baltic Exchange from the Secretary of the London Corn Trade Association regarding facilities for setting up a futures ring on the floor of the Exchange, 19 March 1929

LONDON CORN TRADE ASSOCIATION.

LIMITED.

GRAIN FUTURES CONTRACT.

LONDON GRADE WHEAT.

Lᴏɴᴅᴏɴ,..................................19

....

We have this day **BOUGHT** of you.............000 quarters 2% more or less of London Grade Wheat as

endorsed hereon, at the price of..per 480 lbs. for...tender shipped per Steamer/s and/or Power Vessel/s, including Freight and Insurance, direct or indirect to LONDON or at Seller's option, delivered in authorised Granaries at an increase of Sixpence per 480 lbs. over the above-stated price.

If La Plata Wheats delivered in authorised granary be tendered, the specific duty of 2/- per quarter paid on importation shall be added to the contract price and paid by the Buyer.

This Contract is subject to the Regulations and Bye-Laws of the London Grain Futures Association. Limited, and to the Rules and Regulations of the London Corn Trade Association Clearing House (of all of which the parties admit that they have knowledge and notice), which Bye-Laws, Rules and Regulations shall be deemed, where applicable. to be incorporated in and to form part of this Contract Note.

This Contract is made between yourselves and ourselves as Principals and not by or with any person, whether disclosed or not, on whose instructions or for whose benefit the same may have been entered into.

500-25-8-33—N.N.O.

....

London Corn Trade Association grain futures contract for London Grade wheat

each 1000 quarters. Every day the Clearing House declared an official quotation, from which the prices rose and fell, and against which margins were calculated.

The Futures Market gave a new lease of life to grain brokers. It was not the first Futures Market on the floor of the Baltic Exchange; there had been one in 1897. It was true that in the 1920s people tended to enter the Futures Market who were not generally engaged in the grain business, but that had no detrimental effect either on the producer or consumer, as the broader the market the easier it was to make sales and purchases. The corn trade used the Futures Markets as an insurance. Overseas millers would frequently hedge their flour stocks by the sale of Futures, or when

Seller has the right to tender in fulfilment of this Contract the following Wheats:

No. 1 Northern Manitoba (Dominion Inspection) ... ... ⎱ at 3/- per 480 lbs. Premium
⎰ over Contract price.

Australian (Official Standards) ... ... ⎱ at 2/- per 480 lbs. Premium
No. 2 Northern Manitoba (Dominion Inspection) ... ... ⎰ over Contract price.

Karachi Choice White, F.A.Q. .. .. ⎱ at 1/- per 480 lbs. Premium
No. 3 Northern Manitoba (Dominion Inspection) ... ... ⎰ over Contract price.

64 lb. Bahia Blanca Barletta and/or Russo, F.A.Q. ... ... ⎫
64 lb. Barletta and/or Russo, Buenos Aires or La Plata, F.A.Q. ... ⎬ at Contract price.
64 lb. Rosafe, F.A.Q. ... ... ⎭

62½ lb. Bahia Blanca Barletta and/or Russo, F.A.Q. ... ... ⎫
62½ lb. Barletta and/or Russo, Buenos Aires or La Plata, F.A.Q. ... ⎬ at 6d. per 480 lbs. Discount
62½ lb. Rosafe, F.A.Q. ... ... ⎭ under Contract price.

PORTS OF SHIPMENT:

Northern Manitoba Wheat: to be shipped from a Canadian Port or Ports (including Pacific), but Seller to have the option of shipping from U.S.A. Atlantic ports (including ports in the Hudson River, not above Albany), in which event Seller shall indemnify the Buyer in respect of any difference in the amount of Duty payable and paid upon the goods by reason of the Seller availing himself of any such option.
Australian Wheat: to be shipped from a Port or Ports in Australia.
La Plata Wheat: to be shipped from a Port or Ports in the Argentine Republic and/or Uruguay.
Karachi (C.W.) Wheat: to be shipped from the Port of Karachi.

IMPORT DUTIES: Certificate of Origin Clause (United Kingdom and Northern Ireland).

"In the event of the goods, at time of shipment, being of a class subject to Import duty, but by reason of origin entitled to free entry or a preferential reduction of duty, Sellers must provide on vessel's arrival the means of satisfying the Customs Authorities as to the origin of the goods, failing which Sellers shall pay interest at one per cent. over Bank Rate on the amount, if any, required to be deposited by Buyers as duty or difference in duty, from the date of depositing to the date of refunding. In the event of the Sellers failing to provide such means of satisfaction within 14 days of vessel's arrival, the Sellers shall refund forthwith to Buyers the duty or difference in duty paid, if any, together with interest and any additional expenses arising therefrom, but in such case, on the subsequent production of the required evidence as to origin, the Buyers shall immediately take reasonable steps to secure for the benefit of the Sellers a refund of the duty paid, otherwise Buyers shall be responsible for all losses, damages and interest incurred thereby by Sellers."

there was a heavy flour sale and they were unable conveniently to cover with the purchase of actual wheat, they would insure against a market rise by the purchase of Futures until they could be re-sold and replaced with wheat on a satisfactory basis.

The letter which Stanley Titford, secretary of the LCTA, wrote to James Findlay, secretary of The Baltic on 19 March 1929 asking to be given facilities for a ring and price marking board on the floor of the exchange is reproduced here.

The Futures Market gave employment to many brokers who spent the whole of their working hours on the floor of The Baltic. They did not even need an office; all their clerical work was done for them by the LCTA and they only had to send a

memorandum by hand upstairs to the Clearing House for their
daily contracts to be registered. There was 'switching' and
'straddling', 'averaging' and 'pyramiding', but mainly 'hedging'
which was the forward purchase made without intention to take
delivery as a cover against the sale of 'actual' grain or its product,
flour. There would be the occasional punter buying for a rise and
selling for a fall. But as A. A. Hooker, the doyen of The Baltic
Futures Market has said,

the successful speculator renders a true economic service by correct fore-
casting and is therefore entitled to his profit. The pure gambler as a class,
tends to confuse the issue; the odds are against him in the long run and as a
fraternity gamblers are benefactors to the market only in the added break
which they give it and the subsidy which they invariably leave behind them
when they quit.

The forward or future price of grain, he said, was based on facts,
estimates and sentiment. The facts were trade statistics, the
estimates were expert guesses on future production and consumption, and sentiment among a large body of ill-informed
speculators was very infectious. The Manitoba Wheat Futures
Market at the Baltic Exchange of 1929 was on a very small scale,
and played its part in the function of all markets which was 'to
maintain the continuity of supply as economically as possible'.

In the inter-war period, trade was seriously affected by the pre-
vailing depression and the LCTA and LCFTA were closely
involved in the efforts made by governments, both nationally
and internationally, to remedy the distressed state of agriculture.
For example, under the Import Duties Act 1932 all cereals and
cereal products which originated outside the Empire, except for
wheat and maize, were subject to a 10 per cent *ad valorem* import
duty. The wording of the material clause of the Wheat Act of
1932, dealing with the basis of value for assessment of the duty,
created at the outset considerable confusion and variation in
practice at different ports. It was eventually agreed that the duty
should be assessed upon the last CIF invoice price plus certain
charges. Representations made to the authorities that provision be

made for the conversion of the *ad valorem* into a flat rate duty, chargeable by reference to weight, were not successful.

In negotiations between the two associations and HM Customs & Excise, the latter agreed to accept a certificate in a prescribed form, signed by them, as evidence in support of a claim by importers for rebate of duty – for example, in respect of a deficiency in out-turn, or of allowances covered under the contract. Following similar negotiations, HM Customs & Excise agreed that arbitration and other samples consigned to the LCTA and LCFTA from abroad be admitted free of duty. The importance of such sealed samples reaching them intact and unopened was strongly emphasized.

The LCTA and LCFTA together with other kindred bodies, sent representatives as observers to the Ottawa Conference in July 1932, convened to deal with matters concerning Imperial Preference. The Ottawa Agreements Act provided, as an addition to the provision of the Import Duties Act 1932, for an import duty of two shillings per quarter on foreign wheat (other than Empire) and a 10 per cent *ad valorem* duty on foreign Flat White Maize. Initially the requirement of the Act that, to secure free entry, goods must have been grown in and consigned from a part of the British Empire, created many difficulties particularly for shipments of Canadian grain through United States ports. To resolve these, the LCTA and LCFTA undertook lengthy and complicated negotiations with the HM Customs & Excise.

In 1933 a second Futures Market was created in Argentine Maize, 250 ton lots, CIF terms. This was sited about fifteen yards from the Wheat Ring. Thus on a busy day the LCTA market clerk was obliged to run between markets in order to maintain orderly progress in marking on the boards the business prices as each deal was concluded. Trading volume was reasonable, though overshadowed by the long-established Liverpool Futures Market. The London CIF La Plata Maize Futures Market, to give it its full name, was regulated and controlled by the London Grain Futures Association Ltd, and trading in the ring was confined to members of that body. The contract grade was FAQ Yellow La Plata Maize. Transactions were based on the terms and conditions of the LCTA CIF contract for La Plata Maize Parcels to London. The unit of quantity was 250 tons of 2240 lb each. All offers had to be made in multiples of one halfpenny per 480 lb quarter. The call price remained static until a price variation of threepence was recorded.

The establishment of two Futures Markets at The Baltic was unable to mitigate to any large extent the effects of the economic crisis which swept the world at the beginning of the 1930s. As Sir Herbert Robson, chairman of The Baltic, told World Monetary and Economic Conference members in 1933, there would have to be some restriction of grain production in the great exporting countries before markets could be restored to health. The problems of shipping were not unlike those of the wheat trade – a glut of ships and unremunerative freight rates. Free trade was being hindered by the imposition of enormous tariffs and as a result the corn trade was suffering more than most.

The London Corn Trade Contract had played, and was still playing, a major role in smoothing the wheels of the international grain trade, and the LCTA, based in London, the centre of world trade, made every effort to get trade flowing again in this time of crisis. Never before had the traditional insistence on commercial integrity been more important than now. Great responsibility fell on the shoulders of those members of the LCTA, busy enough coping with running their own businesses, who gave of their time to serve on the North African, South African, Argentine, European and Black Sea, Canadian, Australasian and USA, China and Manchurian, East Indian and London Committees, which had the responsibility of fixing standards of fair average quality, easy enough to maintain in good times but liable to lapse when times were bad. In the 1930s there were seventy different forms of contract, and each Sectional Committee was continually revising them to conform with modern conditions, and prevent disputes ever arising from lack of understanding of where each party's responsibilities, voluntarily shouldered, lay. Tempers rose more quickly in times of crisis and the conciliatory role of the LCTA had never been in more demand. Warranties of quality had to be stricter, not looser; because of the aura of good faith which surrounded those whose business lay in the London corn trade, the London Contract inspired confidence of a kind found nowhere else. As *The Miller* stated in December 1936, 'the close association of the two great industries [shippers and corn merchants] and the friendly kinship established between them have gone far to make the technique of buying and selling grain so efficient and agreeable in operation'. The LCTA had found a formula that worked – and one that could be applied without bitterness.

Much of the credit should go to the full-time members of the staffs of the LCFTA and LCTA who had to operate the complicated machinery which enabled the associations to provide the service for which they had so enviable a reputation.

Hugh Trenchard was the first secretary of the LCFTA, and he was succeeded by W. W. Pigott. Stanley Titford was the third secretary of the LCTA, having succeeded A. B. Gripper who took over from the first secretary Marmaduke Cradock. Throughout the thirties Titford had as his Assistant Secretary one Arthur Henry Hill, a tall, straight-backed individual with what Sidney George has described as a pseudo-sergeant-major bearing and voice. Mr George writes:

When first he was engaged [as a sample porter], he was quick to appraise the situation and to seize the opportunities which to him were obvious. Here was the Secretary struggling to keep abreast of the ever increasing work pressure due to the expanding trade during its recovery after the 1914–18 War with a handful of staff and a minute budget. The dam had to burst – more staff had to be engaged, with more money allocated by member firms to pay them. So, Arthur Henry went into action. He had a small sample storage room cleared and a table, chair, and a few office appurtenances installed, and – the crowning achievement – a large paper notice affixed to the door reading CHIEF CLERK with the name A. H. HILL beneath. It would seem that the sheer brashness of it took the Secretary's breath away – he let matters stand. Anyway, at that time there were only two clerks and an office boy. Arthur Henry was in and he never looked back. He had promoted himself from sample porter to chief clerk and got away with it – his horizons were limitless.

And so it almost proved to be. Business did increase – expansion was necessary; his forecasts had been correct and, additionally, the Clearing was inaugurated. Then came his crown of acceptance – in September 1924 he was appointed Assistant Secretary.

With the newly created status came the task of interviewing prospective staff: he was in his element. With millions unemployed, any employer in those days held all the cards including five aces. Many and varied were his exploits thereafter: he flannelled his way through many a situation that would have daunted a lesser mortal. He remained for fifteen years.

Another character of these times was Tom Wenden. He had been a sailor for most of his life, mostly in sailing ships – a tough, strong, simple man of the sea who had been beached when sailing ships had finally been ousted. He had an innate sense of humour and could stand any amount of leg-pulling; especially about his ultra-large shiny bald head which the wags declared was polished daily with Ronuk. Soon after his engagement as a sample porter he amazed everyone by appearing in the Arbitration Room carrying a hundredweight bag under *each* arm and with another balanced across his bald head. He explained that the trolley was not available. When the arbitrators and others exclaimed at his feat of strength, he said it was nothing – some natives out in the Far East unloaded ships in that way and thought nothing of it. In the basement sample rooms one of his duties was to keep the shelving whereon the samples were stored in good order: to Tom that meant only one thing – they had to be dealt with as a ship's wooden deck would be, and that was something he understood and knew how to do.

Sidney George summed up Tom Wenden when he said, 'to the LCTA he was a real acquisition, and it was a sad day when he could no longer stand being ashore and went off to sea again'.

The staff operated of course under the direction of the president who constantly changed. From 1927 to 1929 it was the heavily built, stolid Henry L. Routh of Payne & Routh; from 1930 to 1931 it was the quiet, purposeful H. S. Shipton; from 1932 to 1935 Sir Herbert T. Robson; from 1935 to 1937 W. Charles Lamarque.

One of the most outstanding arbitrators of the 1930s was Sir G. Walter Roffey, who could be said to be the first of the professional arbitrators. He was engaged in no other business. By

GINSBURY

Sir Herbert Robson, KBE, President of the
London Corn Trade Association, 1932–5

virtue of the concentration he gave this work he rapidly built up a large clientele. He was a man of the highest integrity and his reputation soon spread. Those who found they had a dispute on their hands switched arbitrations which had previously been carried out in foreign countries to London with the request that Sir Walter should act for them.

Sidney George, who has supplied all this information, has an amusing story of this time about The Pigeons.

It so happened, on a warm day in the early nineteen thirties, there was to be a Standard Mixing Committee in respect of Argentine shipments. The particular shipment month had been a record one and there were hundreds of little round bowls holding specimens of each such cereal, grain, seed, pulse or offal concerned, each bearing a ticket stating the details of the sample. Every inch of every bench contained serried ranks of such bowls, and the side benches were piled high with others waiting to be set out on bench No. 1 when the present lay-out there had been dealt with; and again more for Bench No. 2 and so on until all had been dealt with.

The staff had spent several days in the preparation of this display, a task requiring complete accuracy, and that morning had been hurriedly spent dealing with last-minute arrivals of samples from the Continent. Finally, it was past one o'clock when all was completed, and the staff dashed out to snatch a quick lunch.

During the whole of that morning every movement had been avidly watched by an ever-growing assembly of City pigeons as this bounteous spread was assembled before their drooling beaks – if only they could be invited! They knew from previous experience that it would be courting danger to enter through those invitingly open windows. But suddenly the furious activity of the humans within was stilled. They looked at each other and wondered. After what seemed an age it dawned upon them that the staff had gone, the windows remained open, and there for the taking was a variety and quantity of food beyond their wildest dreams: even their Lord Mayor had never sat down to such a banquet.

They dived in, not knowing which unfamiliar food to sample first and hurrying to do so before the humans returned. They fluttered from bowl to bowl, colliding with each other, squabbling, overturning bowls piled on the side benches and knocking them to the floor. The tempo built up and up and up until suddenly the door opened . . . the first human had returned.

Panic stations. The fellow gave a bleat of anguish. There was a flurry of frantically-beating wings as the pigeons concertedly flew to the few open windows: not all could make a graceful exit from their gluttonous orgy through the limited space, and fat bodies collided and wings scurried to maintain equilibrium. Some crashed against windows which were unopened, and slid down to knock over yet more bowls. The now almost hysterical shouts of the man who had entered did nothing to improve matters.

Finally, all was quiet, the trespassers had at last all made their exits – albeit ungracefully in a lot of instances, and the room resembled a scene reminiscent of Waterloo after the battle. The department manager and the rest returned and each in turn gazed open-mouthed at the scene. The manager, suddenly regaining his composure and realising only about ten minutes remained before the Standard Committee were due, ordered his staff to scrape the samples together into some sort of order . . . and to keep their mouths shut.

The pigeons were lucky in one respect. By the time the sample grain had reached the bowls from which they derived their hastily snatched feast, it had undergone an elaborate sifting. For in the 1930s when Dr Bernard Dyer and Partners were LCTA's official analysts, the records show that there were abnormally high quantities of admixture found in the parcels of grain, mainly barley, which arrived at this time from the Middle East and North Africa. In 1978 Dr J. H. Hamence, the partner who dealt with the samples between the wars, remembered how he formed the opinion then that shippers were more interested in exporting the desert than barley.

3

Forty years of progress retarded by a second World War, boosted by the EEC and topped by the formation of GAFTA 1938–1978

Full government control was imposed when the Second World War broke out in September 1939 (a year in which LCFTA membership had grown to 377). The Cereals Control Board – a division of the Ministry of Food – became the controlling authority for all imported cereals, cereal products, pulse and birdseed. A section of the Board was set up as the Cereals Import Committee, under the directorship of James V. Rank, and staffed throughout by the trade. This committee was responsible for the buying of all the commodities mentioned.

In the early part of 1939 committees were set up in the various port areas in Great Britain and Northern Ireland. These committees, known as Port Area Grain Committees, and which started to function immediately on the outbreak of war, were authorized to requisition all stocks in public stores, also to deal with goods arriving subsequently at ports within their respective areas, and to distribute them in accordance with directions issued by the Cereals Import Committee, and in general to attend to all matters relating to proper reception, discharge, storage and distribution. The LCTA offices were the centre of the London Port Area Grain Committee – the largest of the Port Area Committees.

Controlled firms – those who elected to be so because, as a consequence of control, their activities had been curtailed or had ceased – were remunerated under a 'global' scheme negotiated between the Federation on behalf of the trade, and the Ministry.

In return, the controlled firms were required to place their organizations – principals, staff, and offices – at the disposal of the Ministry. Thus, in effect, they were remunerated for service rendered. The Federation appointed a Remuneration Committee, fully representative of all areas, to negotiate with the Ministry and to decide on the equitable distribution of the total amount paid by the Ministry, on the basis of a base figure for each firm related to its previous trade.

A Food Defence Planning Unit of the Ministry of Food was set up under Henry French (later Sir Henry French) and this made plans with the National Federation of Corn Trade Associations to make arrangements for the import of wheat in war-time conditions. James Rank was appointed to take charge of the whole operation, as chairman of the working committee which operated from his home 'Ouborough' at Godstone. Other members of the working committee were A. E. Hooker (Director, Wm H. Pim Junr & Co. Ltd); W. C. Lamarque (Partner – Harris Bros. & Co.); D. R. Thom (Chief Wheat Buyer of Ranks); Sir Rupert Granger (Partner, Ross T. Smyth & Co.); J. H. Pillman (Partner, Pillman & Phillips – flour importers); W. A. Wilson (Wm H. Pim Junr & Co. Ltd).

Every day the trade was informed that they had to make offers to the government through Ouborough to sell on FOB terms by a certain time. The sellers who made the offers would be members of the trade, some of whom were controlled by the government and some were not. There was a staff of about twenty drawn from the controlled firms. In the port areas, committees were formed from the port associations, including London. Sir Leslie Phillips became Liaison Officer for the grain trade to the government and worked in the MAFF offices in Smith Square. Programmes for shipping were worked out for every commodity to be imported and allocations were made by the Minister of Transport (Lord Leathers). H. G. Turner was Director of Dry Cargo. The trade owed much to the excellent relationship which existed between the Minister of Food, Lord Woolton, and Lord Leathers.

The outbreak of war in 1939 brought a similar reaction to that in 1914. When the LCTA met for their annual general meeting on 10 June 1939 with G. H. Williams, the president, in the chair, members expressed apprehension at the government's action in 'interfering' with their trade by effecting 'political purchases' of wheat from Canada direct (through Ranks and Spillers) without coming through normal trade channels. Williams hoped that in future the services of corn merchants would be used when it came to replacing the security stocks and carrying out any further bulk purchase for the government. A committee was appointed to consider ways by which the present position of intermediary traders might be bettered. When hostilities began in September, the two Futures Markets were closed at once.

When six years later it was all over and peace had been restored, there was no immediate resumption of peacetime trading. Victory had been won at a great price and it took more time than expected to return to normal. As an essentially international organization, when the nations of the world were at war, the LCTA was once more in suspense. Many who had known the way the trade had operated before the war were no longer in business – or no longer living. An opportunity for the pre-war traders to meet their post-war colleagues (and competitors) came with the revival in 1948 of the LCFTA Annual Dinner started, as seen, in 1909. The dinners had been interrupted in the Second World War as in the first, but in January 1948 it was possible to revive them under the somewhat austere conditions imposed by rationing, which allowed the participants a budget meal of sandwiches, sausage rolls and meat pies at a cost of 12s 6d a head.

The invitation which the LCTA had extended to the principal continental associations in 1934, to be represented on their Contract and Standards Committee with full voting rights, was renewed in 1950 and gratefully accepted. Peace enabled the LCTA to resume the international role which was its main *raison d'être*, but only gradually. In spite of a Select Committee of the House of Commons recommending in 1949 that the grain trade should be restored to private channels at the earliest opportunity, control of cereals and animal feeding stuffs continued until 1 May 1953 when the Board of Trade began issuing open individual licences. Full de-control became effective in September 1953 but complete freedom of the corn trade was not immediately attained because of the need to market government stocks.

Grain was the first commodity for which American dollars were granted. Stocks were replaced gradually so as not to disturb the market, and the government's plans for doing this were worked out between 1952 and 1954 with the National Federation of Corn Trade Associations.

With trade freedom regained in 1953, consideration was given to re-opening the London Futures Markets. The question to be answered was, should the pre-war commodities be the basis once more? The consensus of opinion was that this would be inadvisable as the exporting countries had not completely relaxed control, and therefore the London market would not be an effective hedging medium as it previously had been. So the Futures Market which re-opened when the commercial grain market came back in January 1954 was not in wheat, the commodity of the 1929 market which had closed ten years later, since virtually all wheat exports were controlled by government agencies and the normal practice of price formation in a free market was impossible. In addition, the introduction of selling wheat on a 'price to be fixed' basis by the two largest Commonwealth exporters, Canada and Australia, made a 'hedging' market for wheat largely unnecessary. But consumption of barley and maize was on the increase and the sources of supply more diverse.

So instead of wheat, imported feeding barley and maize were adopted with premiums and discounts applied according to the country of origin. The contract unit was 125 long tons tendered from one of the adopted stores, at seller's option; thus the time-honoured use of the quarter of varying poundages according to grain was discontinued. A further milestone in the trade's evolution.

The same machinery was established as before the war with a Clearing House run by the London Corn Trade Association and its London Grain Futures Association with which all futures contracts had to be registered for a fee. Part of this was set aside to build up

The grain futures market on the floor of the Baltic Exchange. The 'ring' where trading in EEC wheat and barley is carried out

a guarantee fund which in seven years had amounted to £20000. Trading was done in the open round the ring on the floor of The Baltic Exchange.

By the end of the 1950s imports of grain into Britain were larger than to any other country, and, though four million more tons of grain were being grown every year in Britain than before the war, an additional seven million tons of wheat and coarse grain (barley, maize and oats) were being imported. Since exchange controls did not restrict transactions in grain, whether physically involving this country or others, Britain had access to offers of grain from every part of the world. Thus buyers had the widest possible choice. In some instances the entire exportable surpluses of grain-producing countries were handled by British traders, and wheat and barley were moved from one country to another, irrespective of their final destinations, by British shippers and brokers. This situation arose because of the known experience of British traders in the handling of their own imports, and because of the facilities which existed in Britain, and in particular in London, for arranging the insurance, finance and the shipping through the concentration of firms in Leadenhall Street and their common meeting ground, the floor of the Baltic Exchange.

The contract forms of the London Corn Trade Association were in common use by 1960 and provided standard terms for the movement of grain from any part of the world to another. The form of their charter-parties and of their liner 'Bills of Lading' were those agreed in consultation with ship-owners, through their representative bodies. Insurance terms agreed with Lloyds underwriters were in common use throughout the trade.

But the 1950s scene was no longer that of the inter-war years. The small millers had closed or been amalgamated into big combines like Spillers and Ranks. Only a few independent firms were left. Each miller used to have his own broker buying for him on the floor of The Baltic but now two or three men did the work of twelve. Later their usefulness was to be further curtailed. This was not because the services they provided as intermediaries were rejected; nor because the cost of them filtered off profits; nor even because of the real advantages of their services as defended by Sir Frank Alexander, chairman of The Baltic Exchange, were denied. The reason was simply the improvement in systems of communications, in particular the long-distance telephone and the international 'Telex' network.

The floor of The Baltic never recovered its pre-war role of the World's Grain Exchange, but the role of the London Corn Trade Association and the London Cattle Food Association became more important than ever.

The National Federation of Corn Trade Associations was a member of the Union Européenne des Commerces des Grains, Graines Oléagineuses, Aliments du Bétail et Dérivés, and the

LCTA participated in the work of the Union through the Federation. The UK delegation was made up of five representatives from the Federation and two from the National Association of Corn and Agricultural Merchants (NACAM). Later this was amended to four from the Federation, two from NACAM and one from the Cattle Food Association, although for some years the CFTA had sent observers both to Union Européenne and COCERAL (Comité du Commerce de Céréales et des Aliments du Bétail de la Communauté Economique Européenne).

W. A. Wilson, a past president of the LCTA and of the Federation, became president of the Union Européenne from 1966 to 1973.

Stanley Titford retired as secretary of the LCTA in 1959 after forty years' service and was succeeded by A. W. Burton, who in due course was awarded the MBE for his services.

Meanwhile for over thirty years Mr G. W. Hawkins, FCIS, was secretary of the London Cattle Food Trade Association. He was also managing director of United Associations Ltd, which provided secretarial services for a number of trade associations.

In 1960, the LCTA and the LCFTA, together with other commodity associations and the Baltic Exchange, were invited to be represented at a conference summoned by the Lord Chancellor to investigate the practice and procedure of the Commercial Court, having regard to the decreasing volume of commercial litigation. In the joint report submitted to the chairman of the conference, the views were expressed that members would always prefer the arbitration procedure laid down in the association's forms of contract to the more costly and time-consuming procedure of litigation; and that the Commercial Court should be maintained to deal with those cases which it was considered essential should be settled by litigation; and that the hearing of cases in that court should be in the hands of judges conversant with commercial cases. This joint report was included in the full Commercial Users' Conference Report subsequently presented to parliament by the Lord Chancellor.

In 1963 the Governing Body of the LCTA became the Council which besides the president, vice-presidents and honorary treasurer included representatives of the main port associations, the National Association of British and Irish Millers, the National Association of Corn and Agricultural Merchants and various shippers' associations.

In 1964 J. C. S. Mackie was appointed Secretary of the LCFTA, though it was envisaged that he would continue to work within the administrative framework of the United Associations Limited. Soon after this, however, it was decided that the association should be in all respects an independent entity with its own premises. Amicable arrangements were made to terminate the long connection with the United Associations Limited, and the association set up its own administration and moved into new premises in the Corn Exchange Building, Mark Lane, where by coincidence the association had held its inaugural meeting in 1906. In 1965 a monthly Newsletter was started.

The LCTA and the LCFTA together with kindred bodies were closely concerned in consultations with the Ministry of Agriculture, Fisheries and Food on the drafting and administration of the statutory instruments under the Agriculture and Horticulture Act 1964, which provided for the imposition of levies on imported cereals. In particular, they were concerned to ensure that the arrangements made for the registration of contracts and for the advance fixing of levies did not impede established trade practices; and also to establish, in conjunction with HM Customs & Excise, mechanisms for resolving day-to-day problems arising out of the interpretation and operation of regulations.

On the Futures Market barley of a specified grading was initially employed at the start of trading in January 1964, and home-grown wheat was added in June 1965. Their predecessors, imported barley and maize, were phased out in July 1965 and December 1967 respectively.

The first annual turnover in home-grown barley was 236000 long tons, and for home-grown wheat in the following year 68000 long tons: these figures have been increased year by year until in the 1975/6 period the tonnage exceeded three million

Harvesting wheat

tons for barley and five million for wheat. Starting with trading in the delivery month of September 1973 the contract was changed to embrace European Economic Community barley and wheat, provided it was tendered from an approved store within the mainland of Great Britain.

The two markets maintained a varied annual turnover during the next decade, barley averaging 750000 tons and maize 150000. (The present turnover in EEC barley and wheat amounts to over eight million tons in a year.)

During these years British farmers had greatly increased their production, and it became apparent that there was a potential demand for a Futures Market, so long as buyers and sellers could be persuaded to accept it as an essential adjunct to their established trading methods. Full consultation with the National Association of Corn and Agricultural Merchants took place, in particular with Gordon Wood of the Formation Committee. To overcome the problem of creating delivery points required to comply with an 'Ex Store' contract, A. A. Hooker proposed using the former wartime stores known as the Recommissioned Mills that were scattered around the country, and had been managed by Approved Service Operators. After much time spent in travelling to inspect these stores, after many committee meetings, and much lengthy correspondence, they were finally adapted for the purpose.

The Home-Grown Futures Market was in business.

The reorganized LCTA had a membership of 363 companies and partnerships in 1964 of which 228 were in the UK and 135 overseas – A. E. ('George') Saville had succeeded A. W. Burton as Secretary in 1962. As W. A. Wilson, LCTA president in that year, said of the 1964 membership,

These include the leading grain firms of the world, residing in every grain centre of the UK and Continent, and some may be found as far afield as North and South America, Australasia and Japan. It is in no sense a close corporation; subject to one essential qualification, membership is open to any firm of any nationality. The essential qualification is 'commercial integrity'. It exacts no bond from its members to trade and trade only in this or that particular way, and it renders those services which it is required to render, equally to members and non-members. However, it must not be thought that, even under existing conditions, there are no advantages in membership. On the contrary, there are many, one of which in particular is the payment by non-members of additional fees and charges for the various services rendered by the Association.

The following year the London Cattle Food Trade Association dropped the 'London' from its title and invited the kindred associations in Antwerp, Copenhagen, Hamburg, Paris and Rotterdam, to appoint representatives to attend meetings of the Council and to participate fully in its discussions. In 1968 similar invitations were extended to Dublin, Milan and Zürich and the articles of association were amended to provide that there should be a vice president elected by the Council from nominations received from associations outside the United Kingdom.

For sixty-five years the LCTA and CFTA had run on separate, but parallel, courses; each association had its own Contracts and Committees elected to deal with appeals against arbitration awards under the conditions of each association's forms of contract. Other committees included those set up for General Purposes, Finance, Liaison with Governments, Legislation, and the Sectional interests of the members such as those of shippers, receivers (mainly compounders), and brokers.

Both were international contract-making associations whose forms were widely used throughout the world in international sales of grain and feeding stuffs, and both had important responsibilities to the trade within Britain. With the re-grouping of the trade – the merger of Joseph Rank with Hovis and McDougall in January 1962 had been a major step in this direction – many member companies now dealt both in grain and feeding stuffs (Spillers and Ranks had done so for some time), and it was felt that considerable duplication of work could be avoided by the

A quality arbitration in progress

two associations becoming one, with uniform contract terms and arbitration rules.

Since there was no longer a real need for the existence of two separate associations with such similarity of objects, in 1969 talks between the officers of the two associations were formally opened. A Joint Committee was appointed consisting of:

	CFTA	*LCTA*
Presidents	A. R. Robinson	E. Strange
Vice-Presidents	K. M. Spence	H. E. Johnston
	R. B. Kersey	J. A. C. Hosegood
Past President	M. C. Mynard	
Secretaries	J. C. S. Mackie	A. E. Saville
		(later W. J. Englebright)

At the outset the committee agreed in principle to an amalgamation, and a programme of five years was envisaged for the complete integration. Events, however, speeded up the process. This was largely due to the amount of goodwill which existed and to the hard work of the committee. The committee's report was issued to all members of both associations towards the end of 1970 and a referendum was carried out to obtain their views. All but a very few were wholeheartedly in favour.

On 31 March 1971, therefore a new, joint organization was formed, The Grain and Feed Trade Association (GAFTA) – incorporated as a company limited by guarantee. On 10 June 1971, Extraordinary General Meetings were held by both the LCTA and CFTA at which the following resolutions were passed unanimously:

That the Council be and they are hereby authorised to enter into and execute an Agreement and Deed of Assignment for the transfer of the Association's property, undertaking and assets to The Grain and Feed Trade Association Limited jointly with the LCTA/CFTA [whichever was the case] in the form of the draft document produced to the meeting and for the purposes of identification signed by the Chairman.

and

That it is in the interest of the members that the undertaking of the Association be merged with that of the LCTA/CFTA by transferring the same to a company formed for this purpose called The Grain and Feed Trade Association Limited.

An inaugural luncheon was held at the Innholders' Hall on the 11 June 1971.

The two associations continued to work separately, but closely, for another six months when GAFTA assumed the responsibilities of both the former associations and the staff of the CFTA moved into the offices in the Baltic Exchange Chambers which GAFTA now occupies. H. E. Johnston of Bunge & Co., the last President of the LCTA and a member of the CFTA Council, was elected President of the new association.

Under the transitional arrangements the first President was to hold office for two years, thereafter the term would normally be one year. The Council was to include all members of the Council of the two former associations. There were separate committees for Cereals and Proteins as well as a General Purposes Committee. But within two years the Cereals and Proteins Committees were found to be no longer necessary and the committee structure was revised on the following lines: General Purposes; Finance;

The UK, European and Black Sea Committee making up standards. Left to right, *Mrs L. Withers, C. Donaldson, J. Jackson, G. Caruana, G. W. Richards, C. E. A. Blackmore, R. T. Jeffery, W. H. Defoe and G. W. Swain*

Section Committees – (shippers, receivers, brokers, marine and animal products etc.). In 1976 the Pulse Committee was added.

It was essential that the new association should have a unified system of contracts and its own Arbitration Rules. The rules of the two associations had to be combined to become the new GAFTA Rules before the amalgamation became effective. This work was carried out by a special Sub-Committee. The question of the contracts was not quite so urgent, because in practice the existing contracts were either for cereals or for proteins, and only in a few cases did the contract numbers overlap. The Contracts Committee, however, lost no time in rationalizing the standard clauses.

On 1 October 1971 GAFTA took over all the duties, assets and responsibilities of both the LCTA and CFTA. (The LCTA was finally wound up on 15 May 1972.) The combined association had a membership of some 600 companies in Britain and overseas, with joint net assets of £81600 and an annual subscription income of £17000. The merger helped to consolidate London as the centre of international grain and cattle food trade, the source from which international forms of contract emanated, and the seat of arbitration conducted under British law with the aid of British brokers conversant with its technicalities. Some seventy GAFTA standard contract forms were formulated – a few in French as well as English. J. C. S. Mackie was appointed secretary general (since 1972 director-general), and W. J. Englebright who had been appointed assistant secretary of the London Corn Trade Association in 1970 became assistant secretary general (since 1972 secretary). In 1976 Mrs P. M. Croft, who had been on the staff of the CFTA and was one of the first ladies to have been elected to the Baltic Exchange, was appointed assistant secretary.

As the successor of the London Corn Trade Association, GAFTA took over the London Grain Futures Association. The Futures Market for CIF imported maize and barley, started on The Baltic in 1954, had been discontinued in 1964 and gave way on 1 June, as seen, to home-grown barley, and on 5 July 1965, to home-grown wheat. 'Spot' trading in actual imported grain continued at the London Corn Exchange and in grain dealers' offices.

W. J. Englebright,
Secretary of GAFTA

Mrs P. M. Croft,
Assistant Secretary of GAFTA

From 1 October 1971, the London Grain Futures and Clearing House Committee of GAFTA ran the futures trading on The Baltic, the machinery and procedures remaining the same. Most farmers began each year hoping their crops would be high quality 'milling' wheat and barley of the kind that attracted the higher price, but by the time the weather had done its worst the samples they were able to present to the millers fell very short of their expectations. Quantity remained about the same from year to year, but the quality never. A varying amount of every wheat crop turned out to be of the poorer quality classed as 'feed' wheat only acceptable to the compounder. Only a proportion of the barley was good enough for the maltster. Much of the feed wheat and barley was consumed on the farms where they were grown – at the end of the 1960s about half a million tons of wheat and two million tons of barley – and it was the balance of this animal feed grain which was sold on the Home Grown Futures Market.

As a result of marketing regulations in North America and within the European Economic Community which specified standards for grain, the nature of grain analysis changed. While total admixture was still required, a breakdown of the admixture became necessary together with the determination of the proportion of damaged grain – damaged, that is, by heat, insects and the rest. Examination for insect infestation was also sometimes required. In the 1970s a substantial proportion of the work was concerned with grain grown in the UK, whereas before 1939 samples of English grain were a rarity. The analysis work now carried out by Dr Bernard Dyer and Partners* includes malting barley exported to the continent and sold on a GAFTA contract for which germination, sieving, moisture and protein tests are required.

It was realized that Britain's entry into the European Economic Community and the application of the Common Agricultural Policy to her trade, was going to constitute a minor revolution in the grain trade, in which the services of GAFTA as an inter-

* Dr Dyer died in 1948 aged ninety-three.

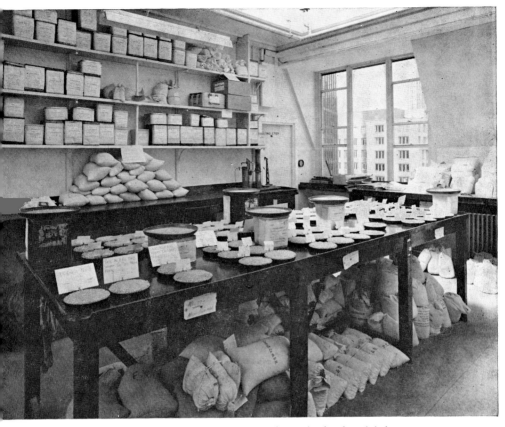

The GAFTA sample room, showing arrangements for overhead and north light

preter and international conciliator were going to be in greater demand than ever before. It involved a great deal of work for the association, not only in conveying to members news of new legislation, but also in representing members' interests and conveying the trade's point of view to the authorities in Whitehall and in Brussels. In respect of cereals and feed stuffs, liaison with the ECC commission is carried out through COCERAL, the international federation, recognized by the commission, and represented on the EEC Consultative Committee for cereals. GAFTA also supports the other International trade federation namely EFAPIT, Euromarket Federation of Animal Protein Importers and Traders, and CICILS (Confédération Internationale du Commerce et des Industries des Légumes Secs).

As James Prior, Minister of Agriculture pointed out at the Agricultural Trade Conference which GAFTA organized in London in March 1972 to consider the functioning of the trade in an enlarged EEC, the existing Community (the Six) was already one of the world's largest producers of wheat. France alone produced more wheat than Canada, though of a different kind. When the Community was enlarged to Nine the compounding capacity would increase by more than a third. He welcomed the calling of the conference since, with such an important agglomeration of grain-producing and grain-using interests, they should meet together and open a dialogue on their problems and their exciting future.

And so we look to a future where there will be new challenges and new problems. The Government certainly recognises the particular importance that efficient marketing will have after our accession to the EEC and are engaged at the moment in a close study of the current situation in the Community.

He was glad to see among the speakers M. Pierre Pignot of the EEC Commission.

M. Wijler of Rotterdam, a vice-president of GAFTA, said as Europeans they realized a common agricultural policy, which was one of the cornerstones of integration, would require the sacrifice of some of their traditions, but they had not appreciated it would be made without a proper transfer of power. 'The result has been an agricultural policy that has left farmers rebellious, consumers resentful, the trade strangulated, our overseas friends estranged and the third world distrustful.' The present autarchic structure of the Common Market might have liberalized the Community's internal trade but it had restricted its trade with non-members. If this was not changed it might well work as a boomerang.

GAFTA differed from the continental associations, he said, in that it was a truly international rather than a national organization. In recent years particularly, successful efforts had been made to stress the international character in GAFTA's two predecessors, LCTA and CFTA. Although traders on the continent remained unhappy with certain contract provisions, GAFTA provided a unique international trade forum. It was important that this

The GAFTA dinner, 1973. Sir Henry Plumb, President of the National Farmers Union, proposing the toast of the Association, flanked by Mr H. E. Johnston, President (right of picture), and Mr L. Pullen, Deputy President

forum be strengthened. GAFTA had recognized the role of its overseas membership and given them representation on the Council. This had promoted the exchange of ideas. The continental associations through their secretaries stood ready, as before, to improve that working relationship. He went on to say:

GAFTA has strengthened its secretariat by the appointment of a director-general. It may be worthwhile to consider if the interests of the various trade organizations assembled here today would not benefit from a focal point within or without GAFTA in which a specialist on EEC matters would be appointed to serve your joint interests. Such a specialist could facilitate the change-over in trade practice during the transition period.

His advice was heeded and in 1976 Michael Johnston was appointed Trade Policy Co-ordinator.

Early in 1973, as a result of a meeting held in Hamburg, the Council approved the setting up of an International Contracts Policy Committee with representatives of Belgium, Denmark, France, Holland, Germany, Italy, the Republic of Ireland, and Switzerland as well as representatives of international shippers. This committee meets once a quarter in one of the main commercial centres of Europe to discuss amendments to existing contracts or drafts of new ones.

In 1978 there is a range of seventy-two contracts and this is likely to be extended. At least eighty million tons of goods a year are sold and moved on the terms of GAFTA contracts. The contracts are kept constantly under review and amended whenever necessary to meet changing conditions and requirements of the trade. It was fortunate that the Rules and the Arbitration Department were so well prepared because in 1972 and 1973 there took place two momentous events which were to bring about a great many disputes. These were the serious floods in the Mississippi Valley in 1972, and the United States government's embargo on exports of agricultural products in 1973. As a result there were 1827 arbitrations in 1973/4, and 1500 in 1974/5.

These arbitrations, requested by parties to GAFTA contracts who found themselves in a dispute they could not settle amicably, were both 'quality' and 'technical' arbitrations. Moreover they were 'institutionalized' arbitrations held at Baltic Chambers under GAFTA rules, as opposed to 'ad hoc' arbitrations of the kind mounted by the London Maritime Arbitrators Association five floors below in the same building. In 95 per cent of GAFTA arbitrations, those in dispute were domiciled outside the UK. In 1975 the wide use of London arbitration services prompted GAFTA to organize a one-day Conference on Commercial

The Rt Hon. Lord Elwyn Jones, PC, opening the Arbitration Conference organized by GAFTA in conjunction with FOSFA, June 1975. Seated next to him is Mr B. Mc C. Rutherford, President of GAFTA

Arbitration in Commodity Trades, which they held in a London hotel on 24 June in association with FOSFA, the Federation of Oils, Seeds and Fats Associations. The conference was designed to promote a greater understanding of commercial arbitration as it was applied to commodity trades; to encourage greater uniformity between the practices of trade associations which provided facilities and rules for arbitration; to promote understanding of the effects of recent legislation; to consider the requirements of traders outside the UK.

Opening the conference, the Lord Chancellor, Lord Elwyn-Jones, said he valued the importance of the work of arbitrators and the benefit they brought to Britain by strengthening the position of London as the centre in that international field and by the services rendered to traders everywhere who could bring disputes to them with the confidence of a just decision. He congratulated GAFTA on organizing the conference in conjunction with FOSFA.

Robert Goff, QC, welcomed GAFTA arbitration rules since they established arbitration procedure. A useful body of law and practice had developed about the meaning and effect of standard form contracts like those of GAFTA. The Commercial Court which was asked to rule over a 'Special Case' gave particular weight to an opinion when it was expressed by a body such as GAFTA's Board of Appeal.

James Mackie, GAFTA's Director-General, championing institutionalized arbitration, said the first duty of a trade association such as his was to ensure that its contracts, rules and procedures were unambiguous, realistic and up to date. They must meet the changing requirements of the trade. But Cedric Barclay pointed out that, save for GAFTA and FOSFA, English arbitration was predominantly 'ad hoc'. But institutionalized organizations deserved commendation for their insistence on strict adherence to time limits. A claim under their rules must be lodged within ninety days of the time of shipment, and they imposed a twenty-four-day limit on final invoices. Of even greater merit were the GAFTA and FOSFA Finality Rules which demanded proceedings to commence within twenty-one or twenty-eight days.

A panel of speakers at the Arbitration Conference. At the microphone is Professor Clive Schmitthoff. Left to right, Mrs P. M. Croft, A. C. Braakenburg, E. S. N. Faure, Professor Schmitthoff, Dr B. Mankowski, Robert Goff, Q C, C. Barclay and J. C. S. Mackie

GAFTA arbitrations, he said, were cheap and fees low. But Aath Braakenburg of Rotterdam was unhappy at how, under GAFTA rules, each party to the dispute appointed 'his' arbitrator who was meant to be impartial, but when there was failure to agree and an umpire was brought in, he became an advocate. Dr Dietrich Mankowski of Hamburg thought the enforcement of a normal GAFTA award in Germany would be refused because it did not comply with the rules of the New York Convention. The English idea that the two arbitrators became advocates if they disagreed, said Professor C. M. Schmitthoff, made sense in a quality arbitration, but was questionable in a technical one.

Pamela Croft, Arbitration and Contracts Secretary of GAFTA, explained that the conference had been arranged as a stepping stone to other seminars on arbitration. A special committee had been set up by the Council of GAFTA, she said, to consider revision of their rules and codes of practice. The committee would have talks with members from all over Europe. It was hoped one revision would be to allow GAFTA arbitrations to take place outside London.

As a result of the recommendations of this committee, GAFTA's arbitration rules were overhauled, and the revised set came into force on 1 October 1977. This practical result was reinforced by the prestige, already considerable in this field, which GAFTA gained by the organization of this conference in which another distinguished member of the judiciary took part in addition to the Lord Chancellor, Mr Justice Donaldson. Chairman of the morning session was Brian Rutherford and of the afternoon session Eric Faure, president of FOSFA.

Though GAFTA had operated a successful grain Futures Market for wheat and barley, from the early 1970s many members of the trade were concerned about the extent of speculative trade in forward shipment and delivery of physical proteins, such as groundnut meal, cottonseed cake and latterly soya bean meal. Members, who dealt in proteins and found it difficult to trade in Chicago with the incumbent time differentials and problems resulting from their domestic market, asked why GAFTA could not set up a market similar to the one for wheat and barley. The need for such a market became even more evident in 1973 at the time of the Prohibition of Protein Exports from the United States. As a result of the prohibition, there were unprecedented increases in prices in Europe and subsequently bankruptcies. A very large number of arbitrations resulted. The Council of GAFTA, seeing the trade's need for a futures market, set up a study group with the task of making recommendations to establish such a market. The Council then created a Formation Committee under the chairmanship of Brian Rutherford who became president of GAFTA in the following year. The result was that a new market was opened on 8 April 1975. For various reasons it was decided that this should be a separate association, and it was named the GAFTA Soya Bean Meal Futures Association (SOMFA). The market is now successfully established and running satisfactorily.

In 1974 GAFTA joined the European Commodities Exchanges Association which is based in Strasbourg and organizes a joint trading day once a year in one of the main commercial centres of Europe. GAFTA organized a successful trading day in London in October 1975, and has since participated fully in the associa-

The Annual General Meeting of GAFTA, 11 January 1978

tion's work. In 1976 GAFTA's president, C. J. Tilley, was elected president of the European Commodities Exchanges Association for a period of two years.

A main role of GAFTA is to convey up-to-date and accurate information about all events which might have any effect on the corn trade, whether a natural disaster or national legislation. To this end and to coordinate the association's efforts in promoting and protecting the interests of its members *vis-à-vis* government and other authorities, in 1976 the post of Trade Policy Co-ordinator was created and as seen, M. E. Johnston, formerly an Under Secretary at the Ministry of Agriculture, Fisheries and Food, was appointed to that post.

Harmonization, whether within an association, a nation or a Community, depends above all on personal contact. Members of GAFTA meet together every year for an annual 'Bourse'

James Mackie, Director General of GAFTA

which is held on the floor of The Baltic Exchange in which discussion and the imparting of information plays its part, but the main gain is in human relationships – the social activities, the chit-chat and the greater comprehension of the other fellow's point of view and the nature of his problems. In addition, the tradition of the annual dinners started by the London Cattle Food Trade Association in 1909, as seen, was maintained happily on a more generous scale after the amalgamation with the LCTA and the formation of GAFTA, to a point at which it is becoming increasingly difficult to provide for the numbers anxious to attend. Members of the trade continue to give their support to the Annual Dinner of the Cereals and Baltic Friendly Society – now the Cereals and Baltic Society – and that Dinner has been held annually since 1885. It is attended by most of the principal members of the grain trade.

It is not possible to bring this short history to a conclusion, because the story is not ended. The work of trade associations has increased enormously in recent years. This has been due to government legislation, national and international; varying currency values; to fluctuations between shortages and surpluses.

A trade association exists to serve its members and this it must do in the way in which its members require at the time concerned. A trade association has, therefore, to be adaptable and it must depend upon the support and enthusiasm of its members to provide the presidents, officers, council and committee members. It must also depend upon the professional permanent staff. GAFTA is fortunate in that the amalgamation of its two parent associations coincided with the great upsurge in work since 1971. It is dangerous to predict future developments in any trade matter, but GAFTA has proved itself adaptable as well as energetic, and building on the confidence which the world grain trade has placed in it over the hundred years since the foundation of the London Corn Trade Association in 1878, there can be no doubt it will continue to serve with its traditional efficiency and fairness all those who buy, sell and consume cereals and proteins for man and beast.

Summary of the Main Objects of GAFTA

1 To promote trade in Grain, Feeding Stuffs and Pulses and to support and protect the interests of members engaged therein.
2 To encourage uniformity in commercial use of forms of contract, charter parties, bills of lading, policies of insurance and other such documents. To publish standard contract forms.
3 To provide facilities for the settlement of disputes by arbitration.
4 To make up and maintain standard samples of such commodities as might be required.
5 To promote, regulate and control the London Grain Futures Market, and to sponsor and promote the GAFTA Soya Bean Meal Futures Market.
6 To make provision for a full analytical service for members.
7 To organize conferences and meetings to discuss any matters connected with the trade, to express the views of members to the legislature, public bodies, chambers of commerce, sister associations and others.
8 To maintain a close liaison with government departments, relative authorities and others, and by regular consultation to endeavour to assist in the preparation and interpretation of regulations, etc.
9 To keep members fully informed on all matters concerning the trade generally.
10 To encourage understanding of the problems of agriculture and to increase and improve the service which the trade can give to this industry.

Officers and Senior Staff
of GAFTA 1978

PRESIDENT
D. M. McL. Clark, Henry W. Peabody Grain Ltd, London

DEPUTY PRESIDENT
W. H. Defoe, T. A. Jones & Co. Ltd, London

VICE-PRESIDENTS
P. A. Metaxa, Rank Hovis McDougall Ltd
L. Meunier, SEDIPA, Paris

DIRECTOR GENERAL
J. C. S. Mackie, MA

SECRETARY
W. J. Englebright

ASSISTANT SECRETARY
P. M. Croft

TRADE POLICY
CO-ORDINATOR
M. E. Johnston

COMPTROLLER
G. H. Jones

ACCOUNTANT
H. K. Shapland

Council

ELECTED UK MEMBERS

D. M. McLachlan Clark, Henry W. Peabody Grain Ltd, London

J. M. McKean, Thos. Borthwick (Glasgow) Ltd, Glasgow

P. A. Metaxa, RHM Flour Mills Ltd., London

C. Nottage, Nitrovit Ltd, London

E. F. Roscoe, Alfred Isaacs & Sons Ltd, London

H. Schmidt, Alfred C. Toepfer Ltd, London

D. G. Turner, Continental (London) Ltd, London

W. H. Defoe, T. A. Jones & Co. Ltd, London

A. G. Scott, European Grain & Shipping Ltd, London

C. J. Tilley, Willett & Son (Corn Merchants) Ltd, Bristol

A. C. B. Ford, Millford Grain Ltd, Bristol

G

D. R. Marshall, Mitchell Cotts & Co. Ltd, London

D. Wilkin, Wills & Wilkin Ltd, London

A. H. Harper, Coley & Harper Ltd, London

R. A. Standcumbe, Tradax England Ltd, London

I. D. Stewart, The Overseas Farmers' Co-operative Federations Ltd, London

F. R. Alexander, James Richardson & Sons (Overseas) Ltd, London

W. S. Biggs, Continental (London) Ltd, London

G. L. Clarke, Dalgety Crosfields Ltd, Bristol

N. J. MacLean, The Distillers Co. Ltd, Edinburgh

F. A. J. Morley, John Darling Proprietary Ltd, London

H. B. Newman, Cargo Superintendents (London) Ltd, London

J. B. Ogilvie, OBE, TD, Garton Sons & Co. Ltd, London

B. Mc. C. Rutherford, BOCM Silcock Ltd, Basingstoke

S. T. Sanders, Unimills Ltd, Kent

A. R. de Vries, Alexanders Partners Ltd, London

P. A. Wilks, Cranford Brothers Ltd, Ipswich, Suffolk

L. J. Wright, Pauls & Sanders Ltd, Ipswich, Suffolk

G. B. Wood, OBE, Dower Wood & Co. Ltd, Newmarket, Suffolk

REPRESENTING PORT ASSOCIATIONS

Bristol
B. Fawcett, Dalgety Crosfields Ltd, Bristol

C. J. Tilley, Willett & Son (Corn Merchants) Ltd, Bristol

C. Wallis, BOCM Silcock Ltd, Basingstoke

Hull
K. Busby, Reeson Busby & Co. Ltd, Hull

A. L. McDonald, Tradax England Ltd, London

Liverpool
D. F. W. Wildbore, Czarnikow & Co, Liverpool

C. F. Caroe, Barber & Garratt Ltd, Liverpool

N. Ireland
R. Young, Russell & Baird (Ireland) Ltd, Ireland

G. Richardson, E. T. Green Ltd, Belfast

Scotland
J. M. McKean, Thos. Borthwick (Glasgow) Ltd, Glasgow

D. Scott, Philip Wilson (Corn Factors) Ltd, Edinburgh

LCTA Presidents

1878/80	John Ross	1923/24	H. M. Colebrook
1881/82	Edward Majolier	1925/26	Sir G. W. Roffey
1883/84	Richard Reid	1927/29	H. L. Routh
1885	Edward Power	1930/31	H. S. Shipton
1886	S. W. Keene	1932/35	Sir H. T. Robson, KBE
1887/88	Seth Taylor	1935/37	W. Chas. Lamarque
1889/90	R. J. Duck	1938/42	G. J. Williams
1891	J. H. Tod	1943/44	H. W. Walker
1891/93	E. J. Saltmarsh	1945/46	R. Tadman
1894/95	A. W. McDonnell	1947/48	E. W. Grimsdale
1896/98	W. Bridges Webb	1949/50	Fred H. Woods
1901/03	W. P. Ward	1951/52	F. G. Short
1904	A. W. McDonnell	1953	F. A. Bristow
1905/07	R. A. Patterson	1954/55	L. Hosegood
1908	E. G. Saltmarsh	1956/57	C. D. Maccorkindale
1909/11	S. F. Mendl	1958/59	L. W. Phillips, CBE
1912	A. J. L. Payne	1960	F. C. Smee
1913/14	H. J. Strawson	1960/62	R. J. Paul
1915/17	S. F. Mendl	1963/64	W. A. Wilson
1918	Sir S. F. Mendl, KBE	1965/66	R. E. R. Tyrrell
1919/20	The Rt Hon. Thos. Wiles, PC	1967/68	R. R. Thom
		1968/70	E. Strange
1921/22	W. D. Anderson	1971/72	H. E. Johnston, OBE

GAFTA Presidents

1971/73   H. E. Johnston, OBE, TD
1973/75   L. Pullen
1975/76   B. McC. Rutherford
1976/77   C. J. Tilley
1977/78   D. G. Turner
1978/   D. M. McLachlan Clark

LCFTA and CFTA Presidents

1906/08	F. N. Garrard	1948/49	R. Bolton
1908/10	D. H. Grimsdale	1949/50	B. J. Dixon
1910/12	W. H. Pinnock	1950/51	F. L. Winter
1912/23	F. M. Williams	1951/52	G. V. Tottle
1923/25	W. W. Pigott	1952/53	R. F. Barker, OBE, MC
1925/26	Charles Pinnock	1953/54	R. La Riviere
1926/27	A. E. James	1954/55	J. A. Smith
1927/28	Frank E. Fehr, CBE	1955/56	A. J. R. Frentzel, MC
1928/29	E. Hudson Cowell, OBE	1956/57	John Templeton
		1957/58	H. Madsen
1929/31	L. Lillico, CBE	1958/59	F. W. Martin
1931/32	W. H. Pinnock	1959/60	G. A. Smith
1932/34	Geo. Snelling	1960/61	C. A. Hayley
1934/36	A. E. James	1961/62	M. T. Tozer
1936/37	E. W. Grimsdale	1962/63	E. F. F. D. Price
1937/39	H. M. Munro	1963/64	K. J. Arnott
1939/40	E. Hudson Cowell, OBE	1964/65	R. W. Pirrie
		1965/66	M. R. Barton
1940/41	Frank E. Fehr, CBE	1966/67	W. C. W. Macleod
1941/43	A. W. Brown	1967/68	R. W. K. Nott
1943/44	R. Bolton	1968/69	M. C. Maynard
1944/45	E. Steiner	1969/70	A. R. Robinson
1945/46	R. A. S. Templeton	1970/71	K. M. Spence
1946/48	C. E. Williams		

NFCTA Presidents

1918/19	Lt Col. W. W. Petrie
1919/20	W. E. Bagshaw
1920/21	Sir Sigismund F. Mendl, KBE
1921/23	The Rt Hon. Thomas Wiles
1923/25	H. S. Henderson
1925/26	H. S. Shipton
1926/27	Blake Woodward
1927/28	Henry Hosegood
1928/29	Sir G. Walter Roffey
1929/30	Sir Arthur W. Holmes, KBE
1931	Sir Herbert Robson, KBE
1932/33	J. W. Swindells
1933/36	Col. Wm. Hodson, DSO, MC
1936/39	H. R. Granger
1939/41	Charles F. E. Bulow
1941/47	Sir Edward Redmayne-Jones
1947/48	R. Tadman
1948/52	L. W. Phillips, CBE
1952/57	Lance Willett, CBE
1957/60	E. A. G. Caröe, CBE
1960/62	J. N. M. Scott
1962/64	Gordon F. Williamson, TD
1964/66	R. J. Paul, JP
1966/68	W. A. Wilson, CBE
1968/70	R. S. Cornelius, TD
1970/72	R. E. R. Tyrrell

Index